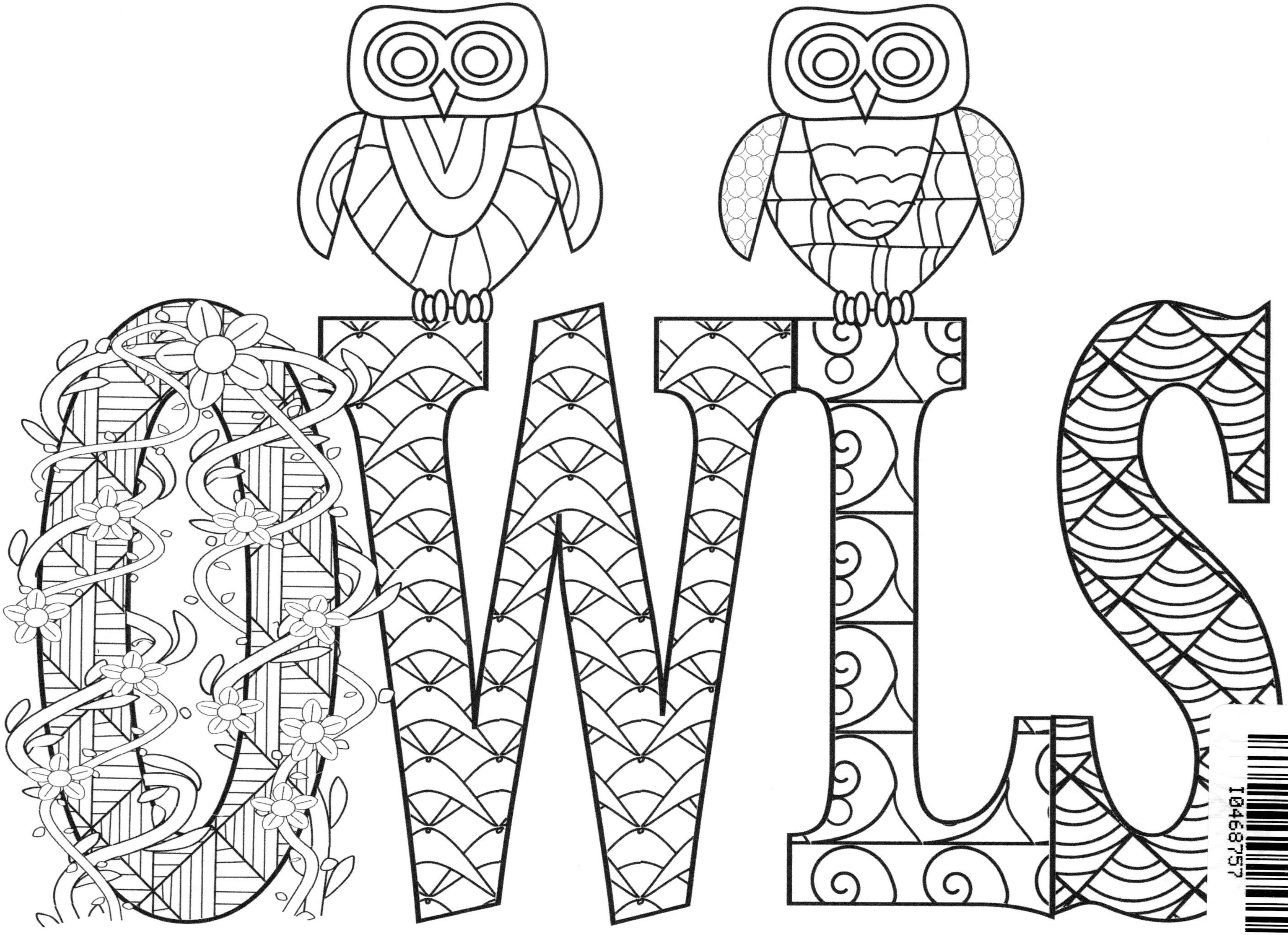
OWLS

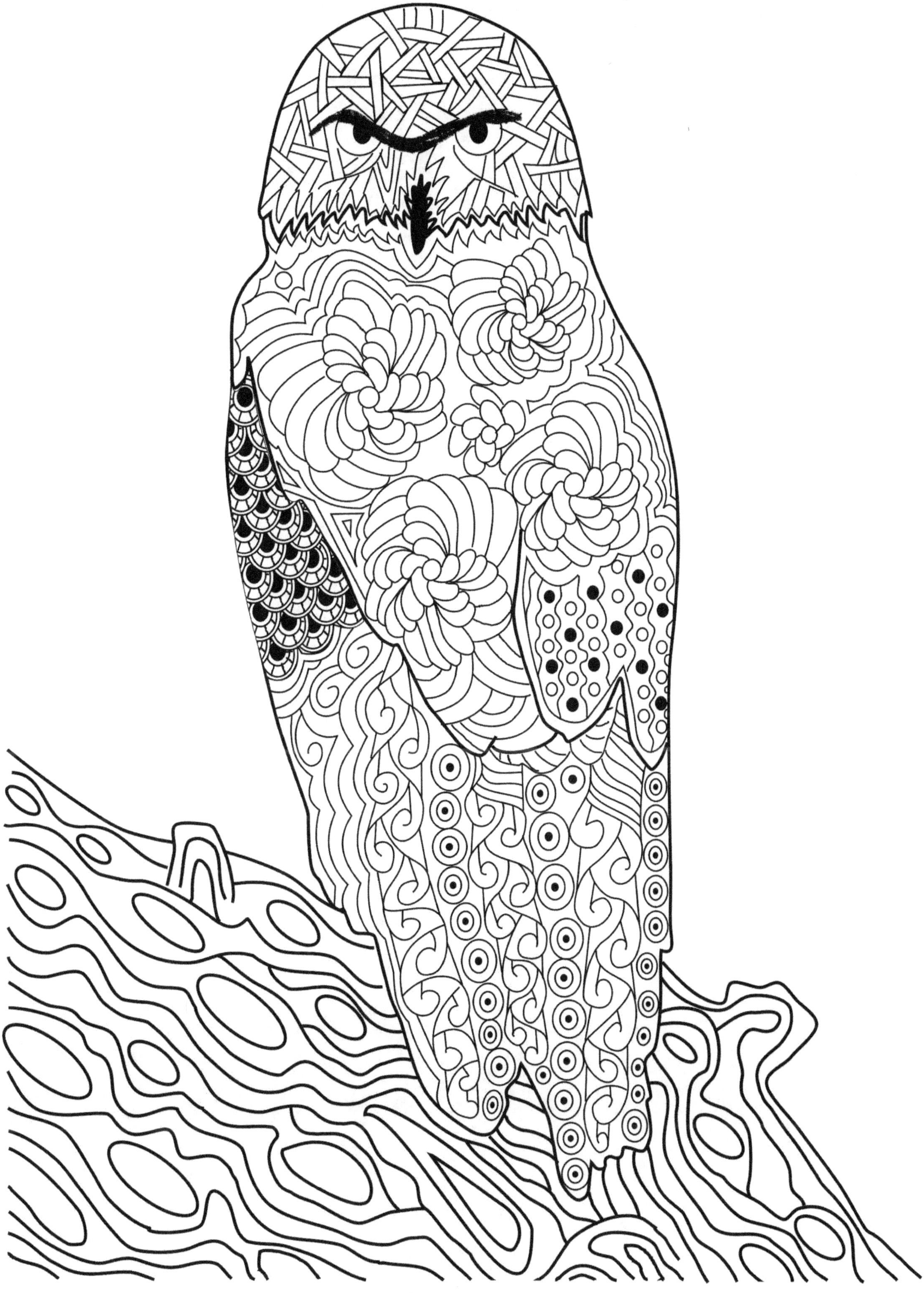

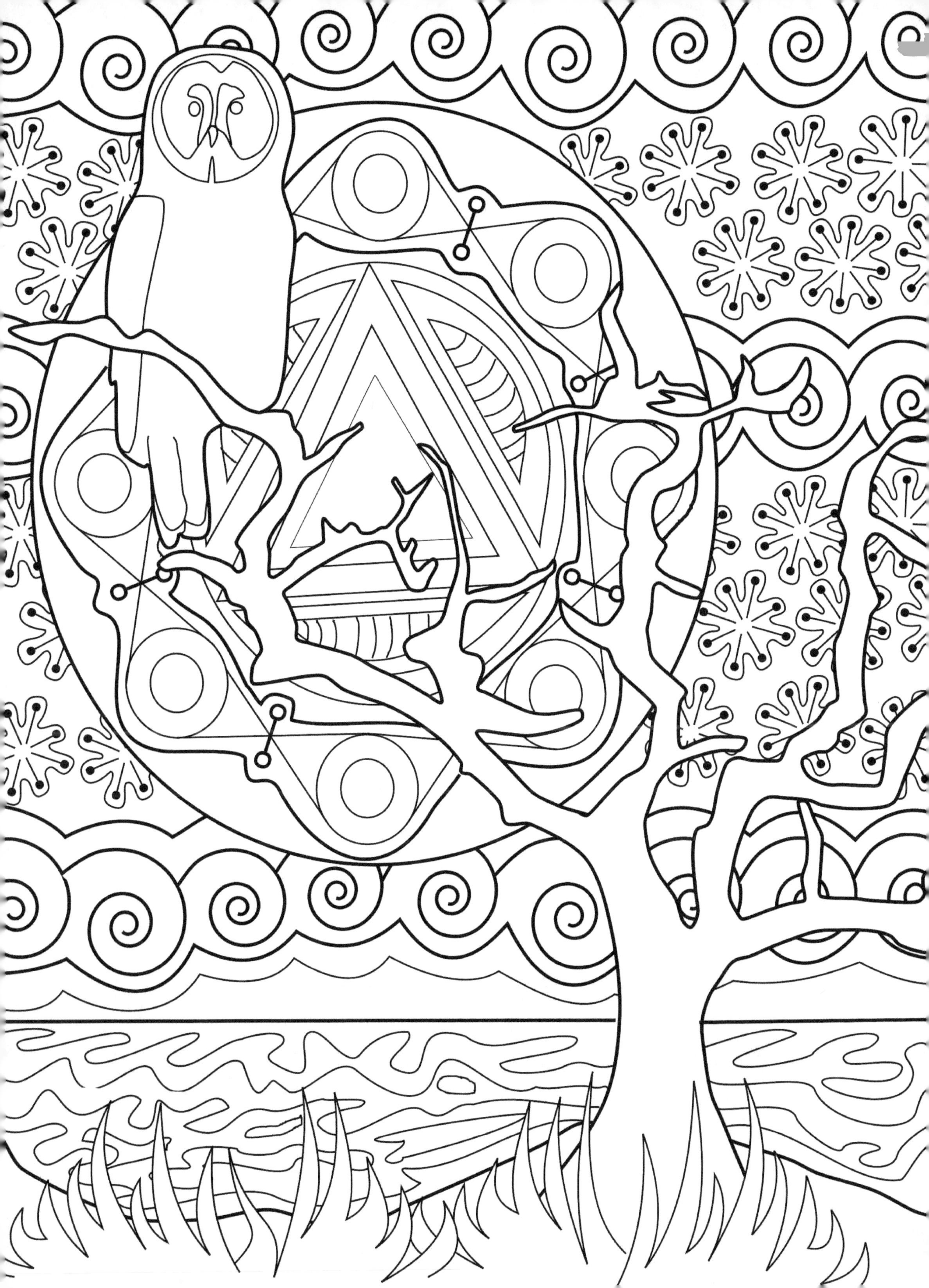

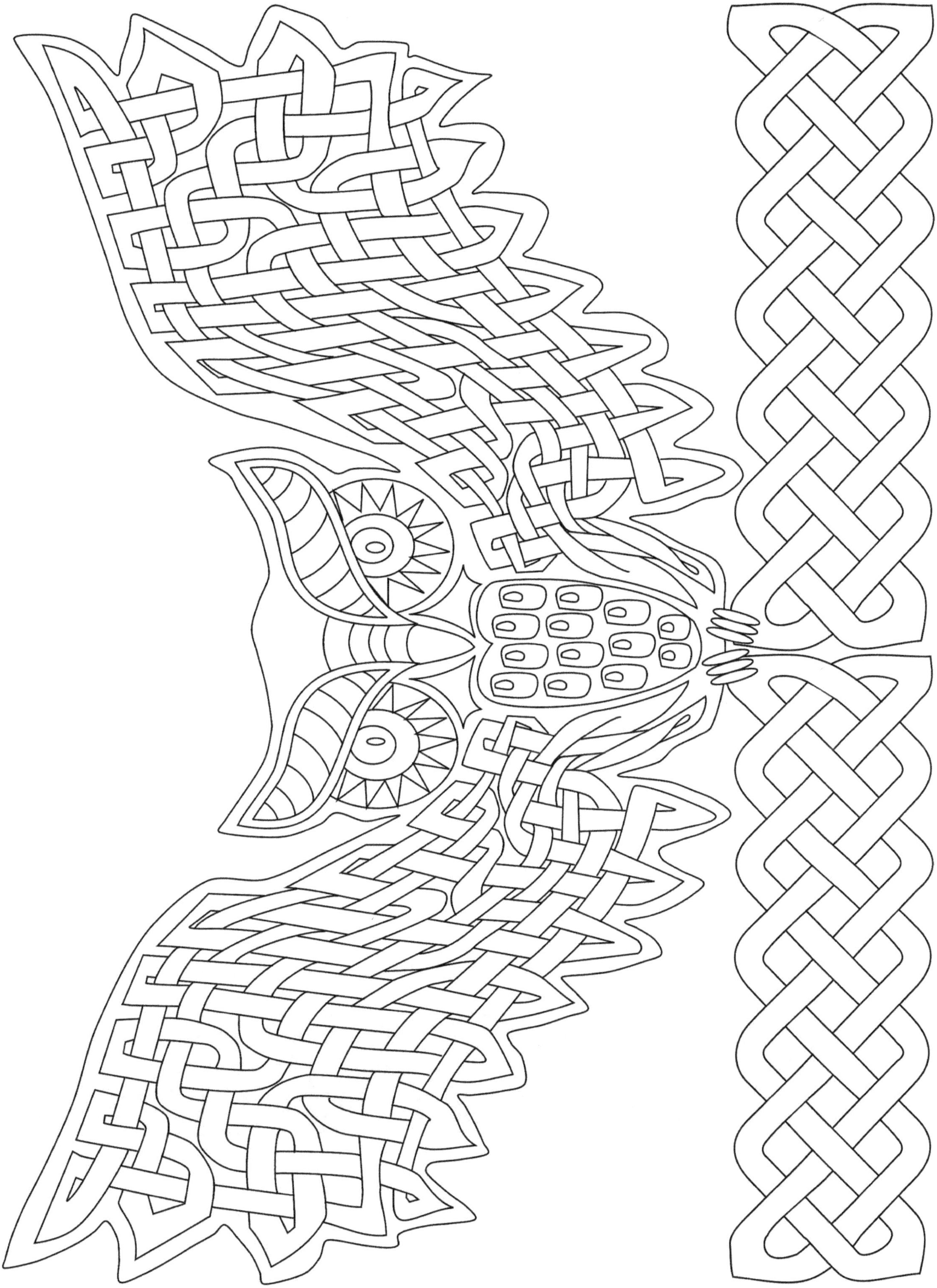

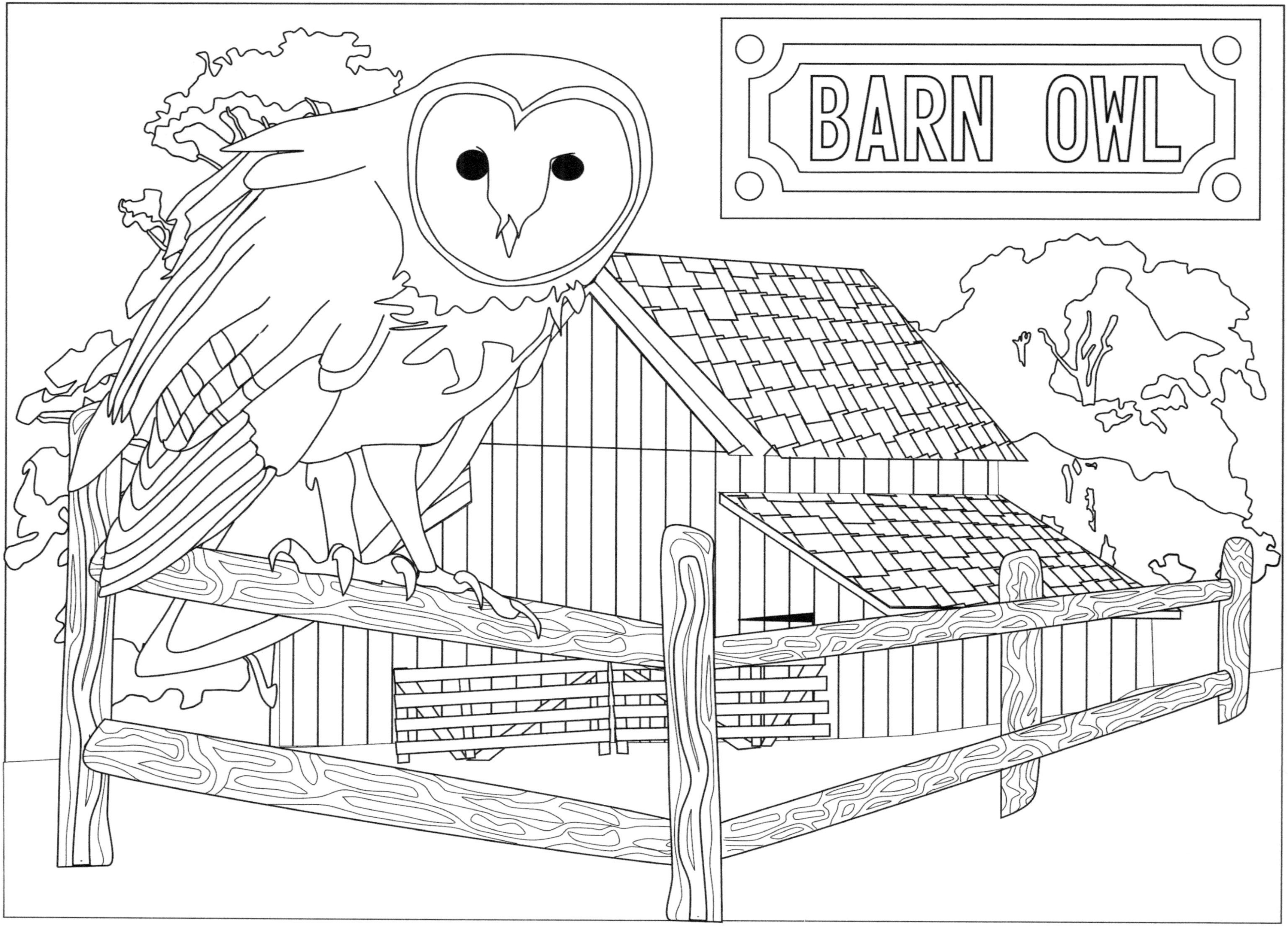
BARN OWL

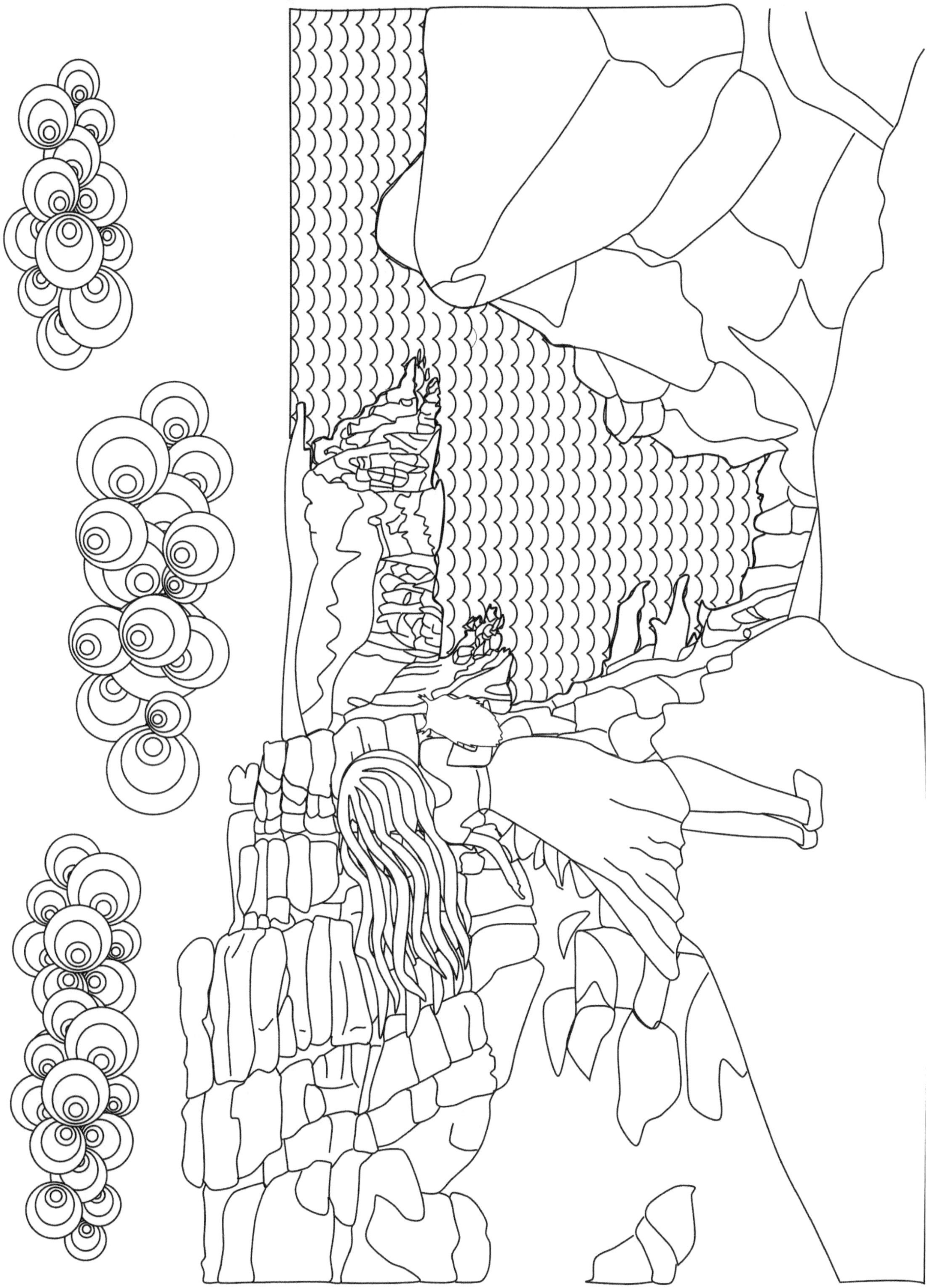

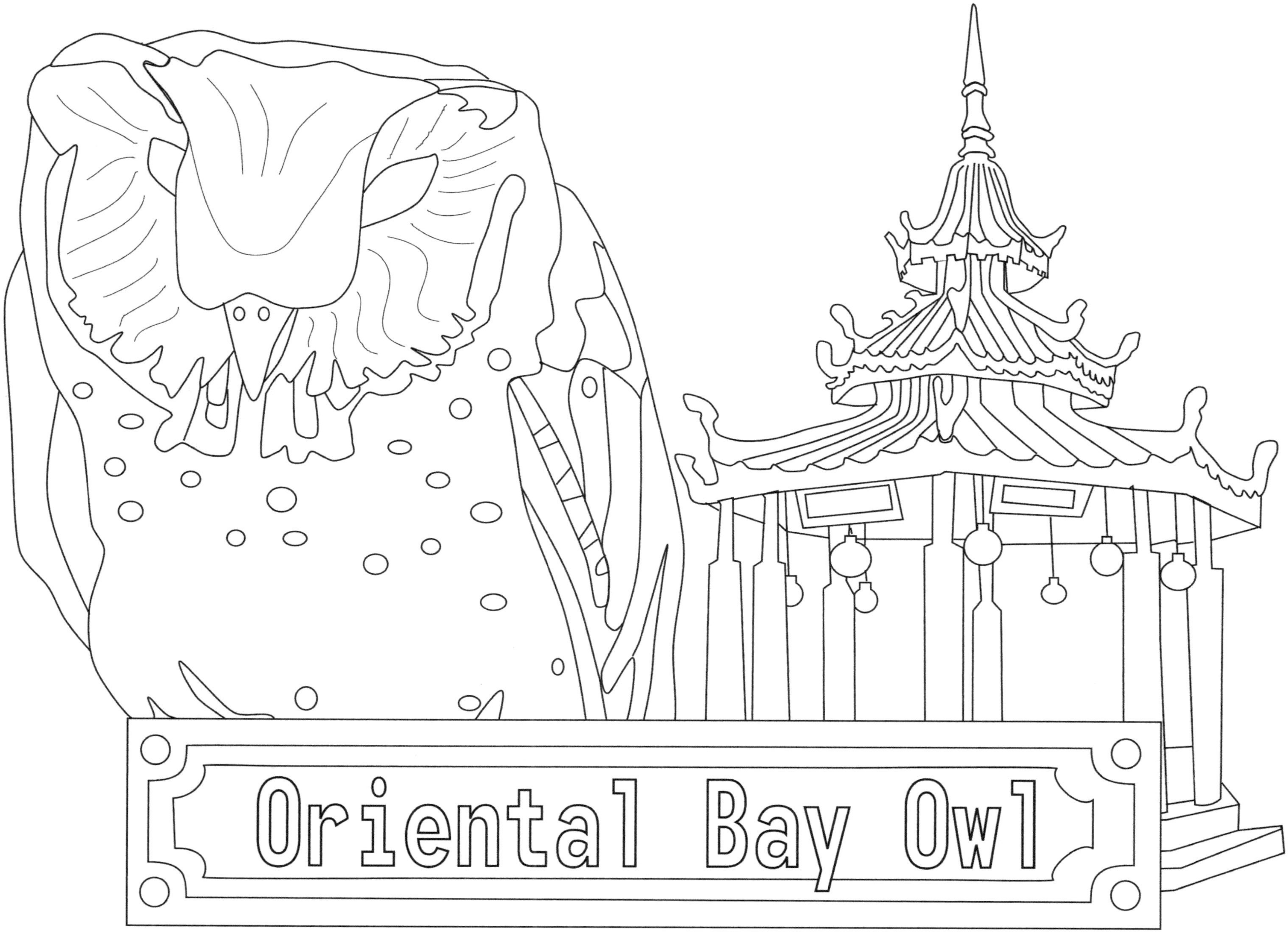
Oriental Bay Owl

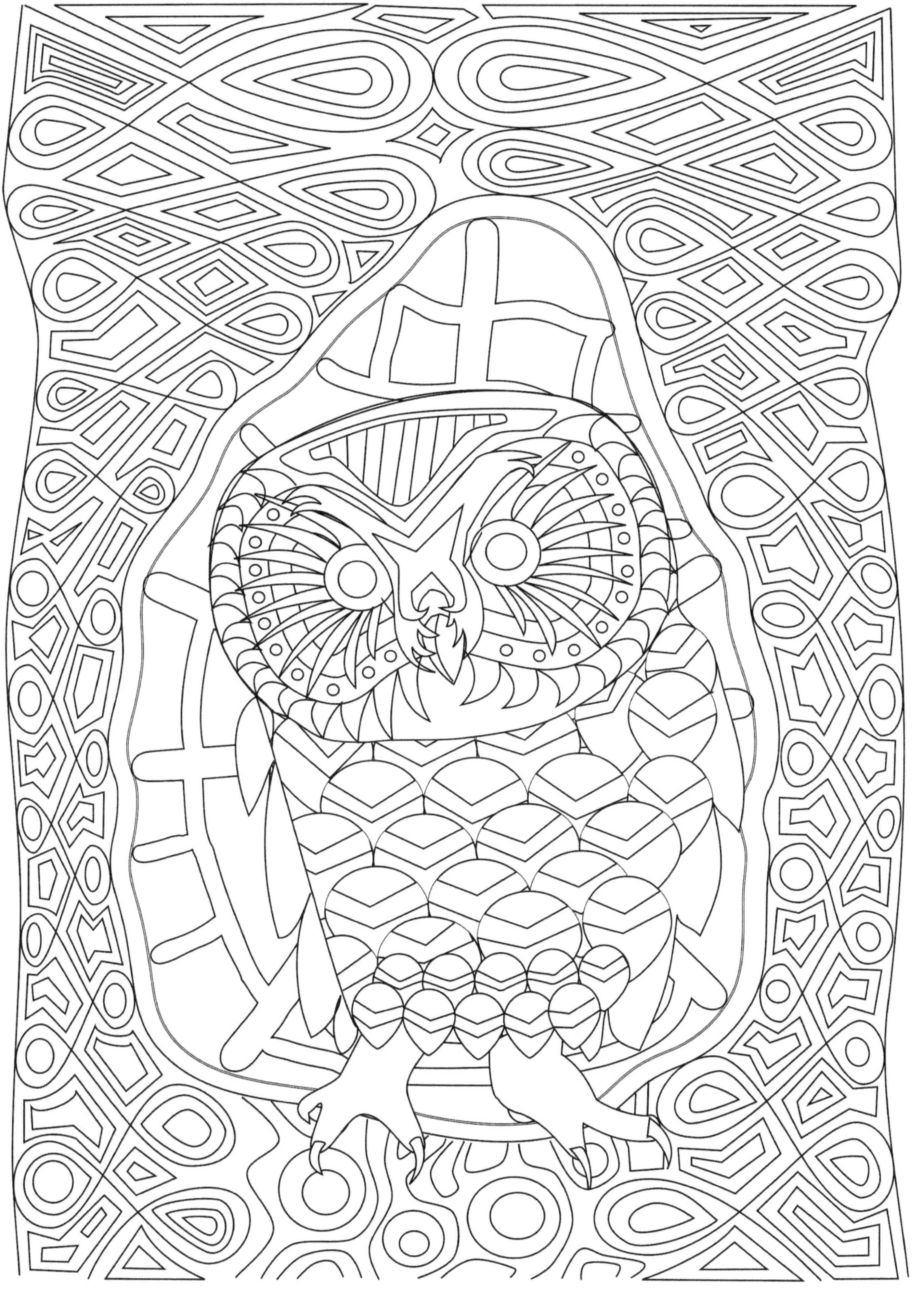

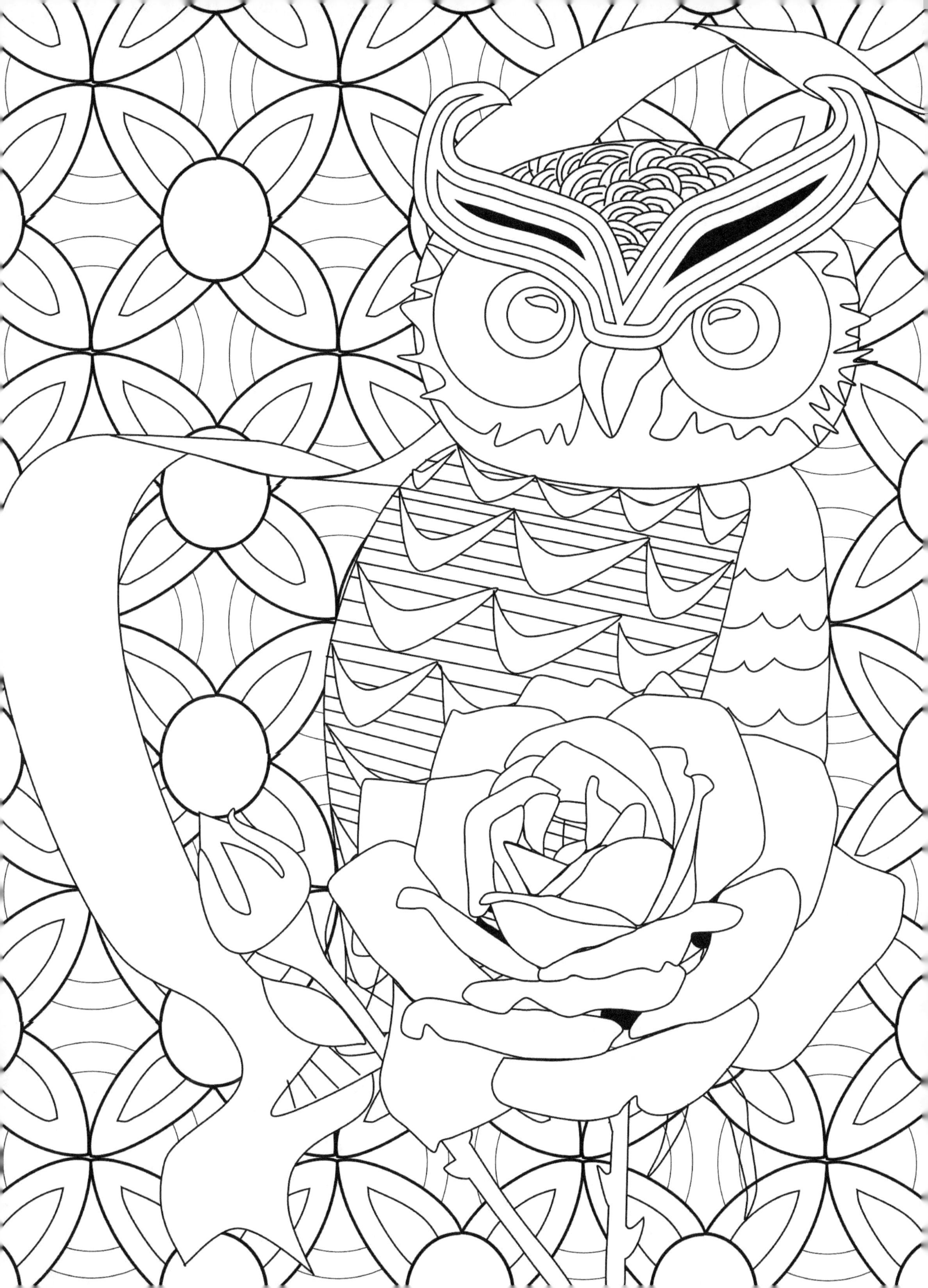

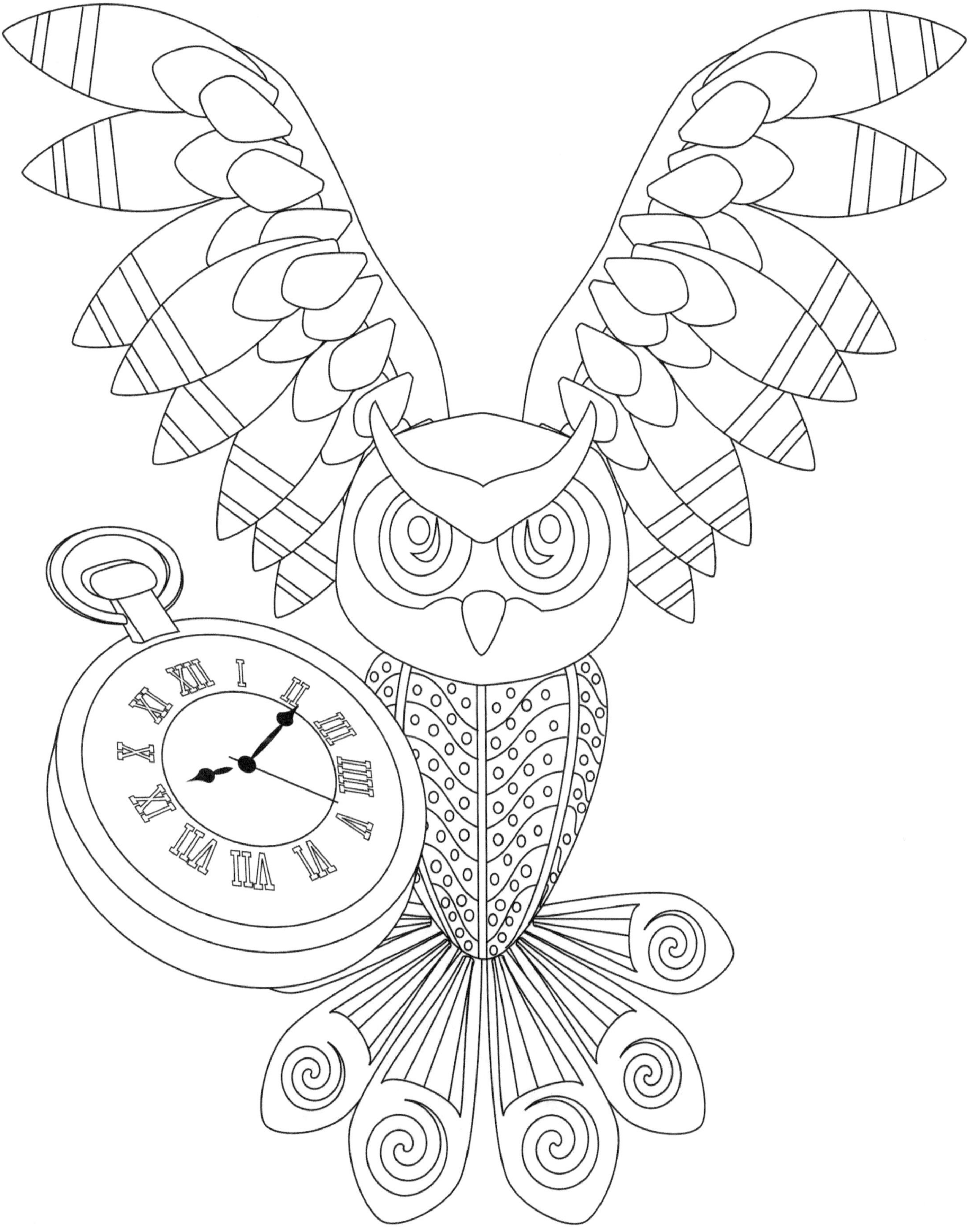

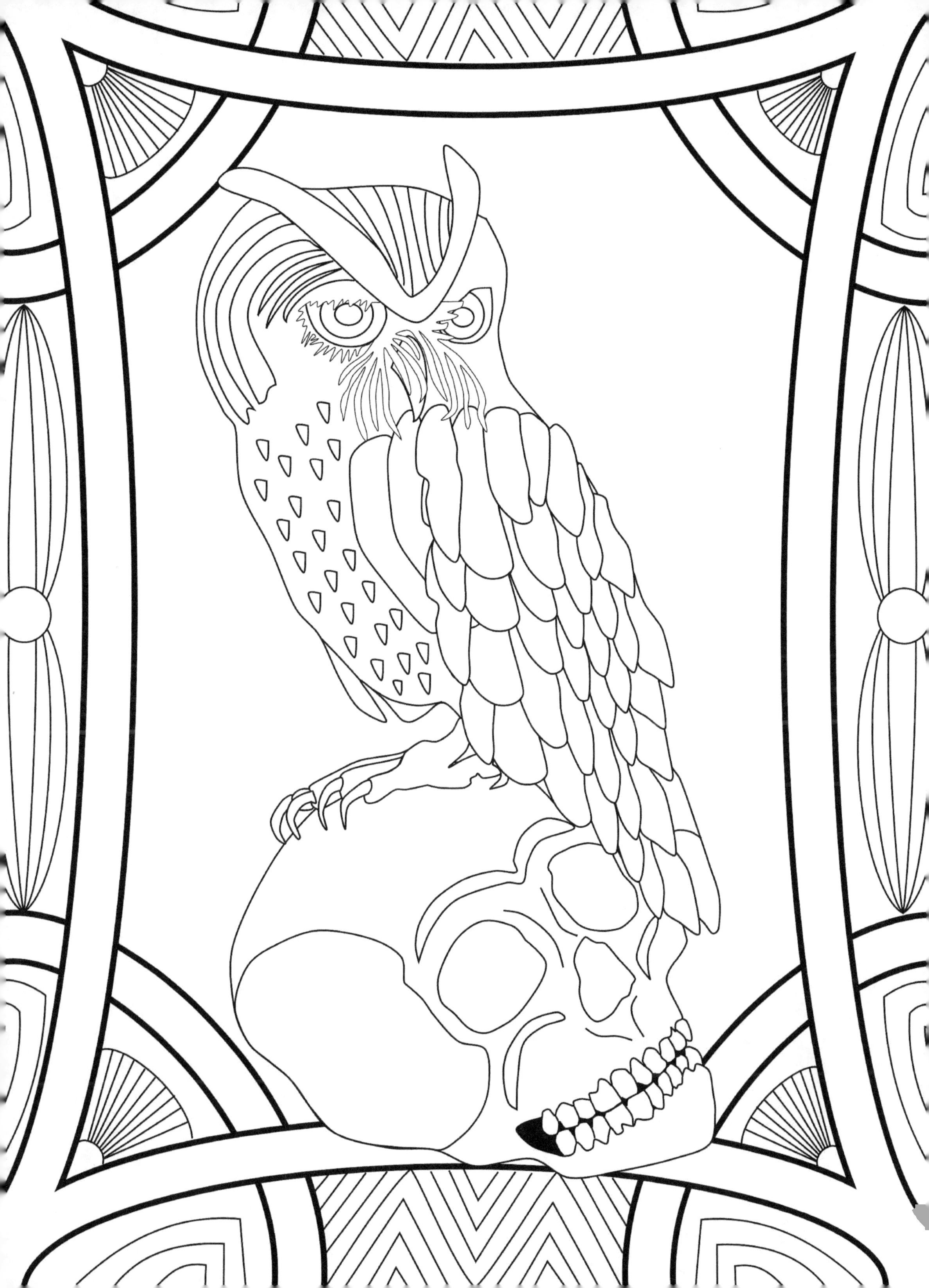

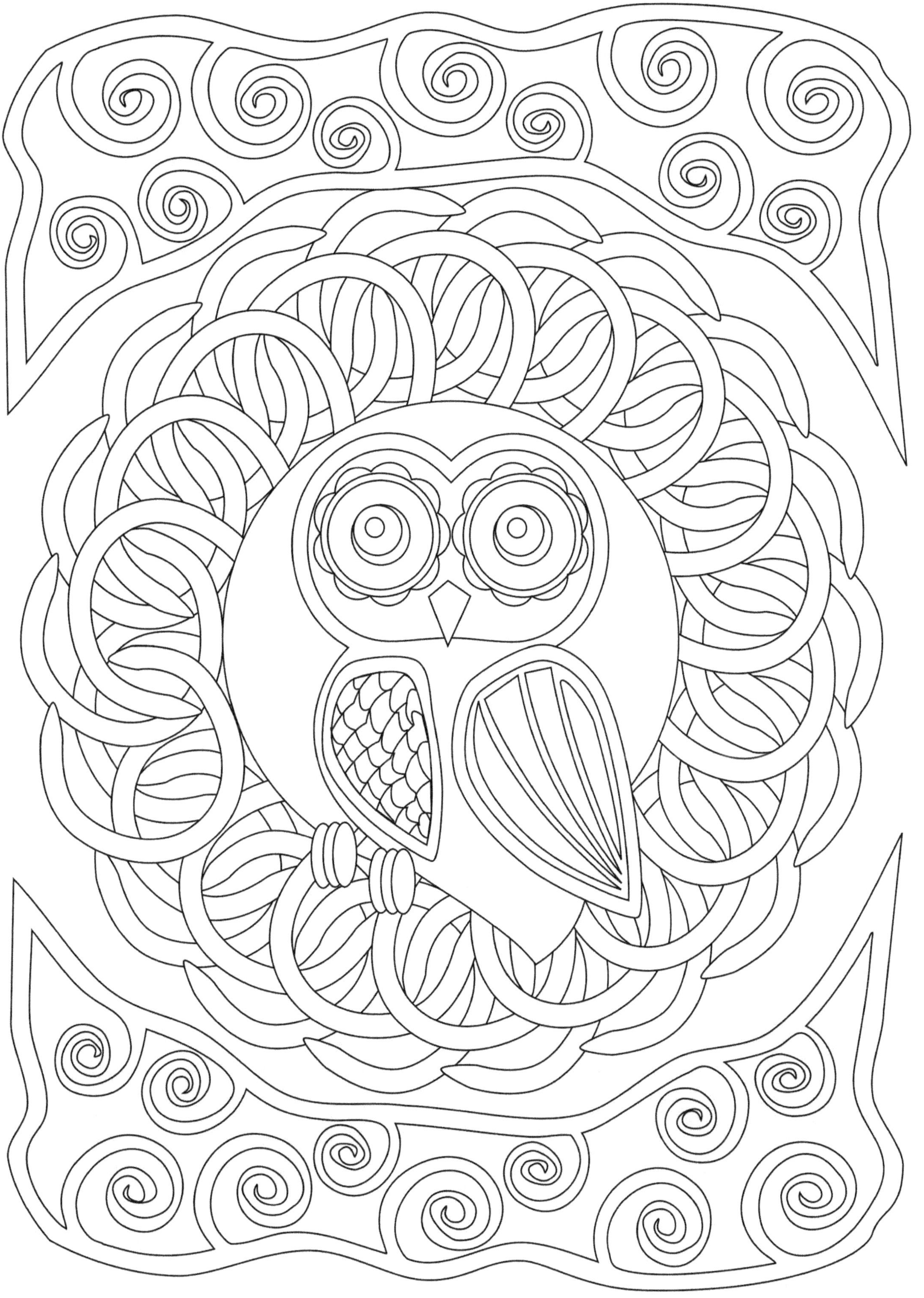

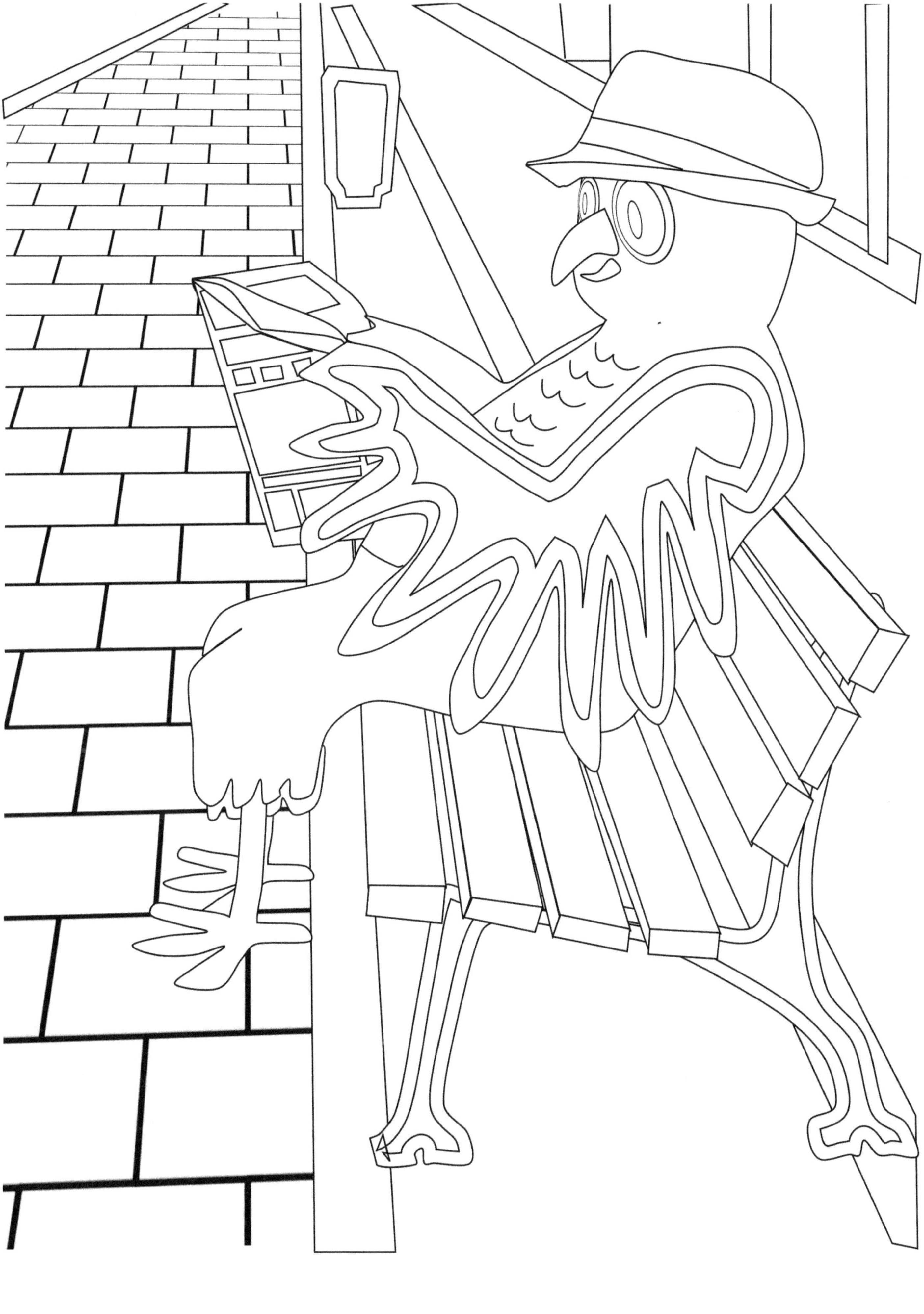

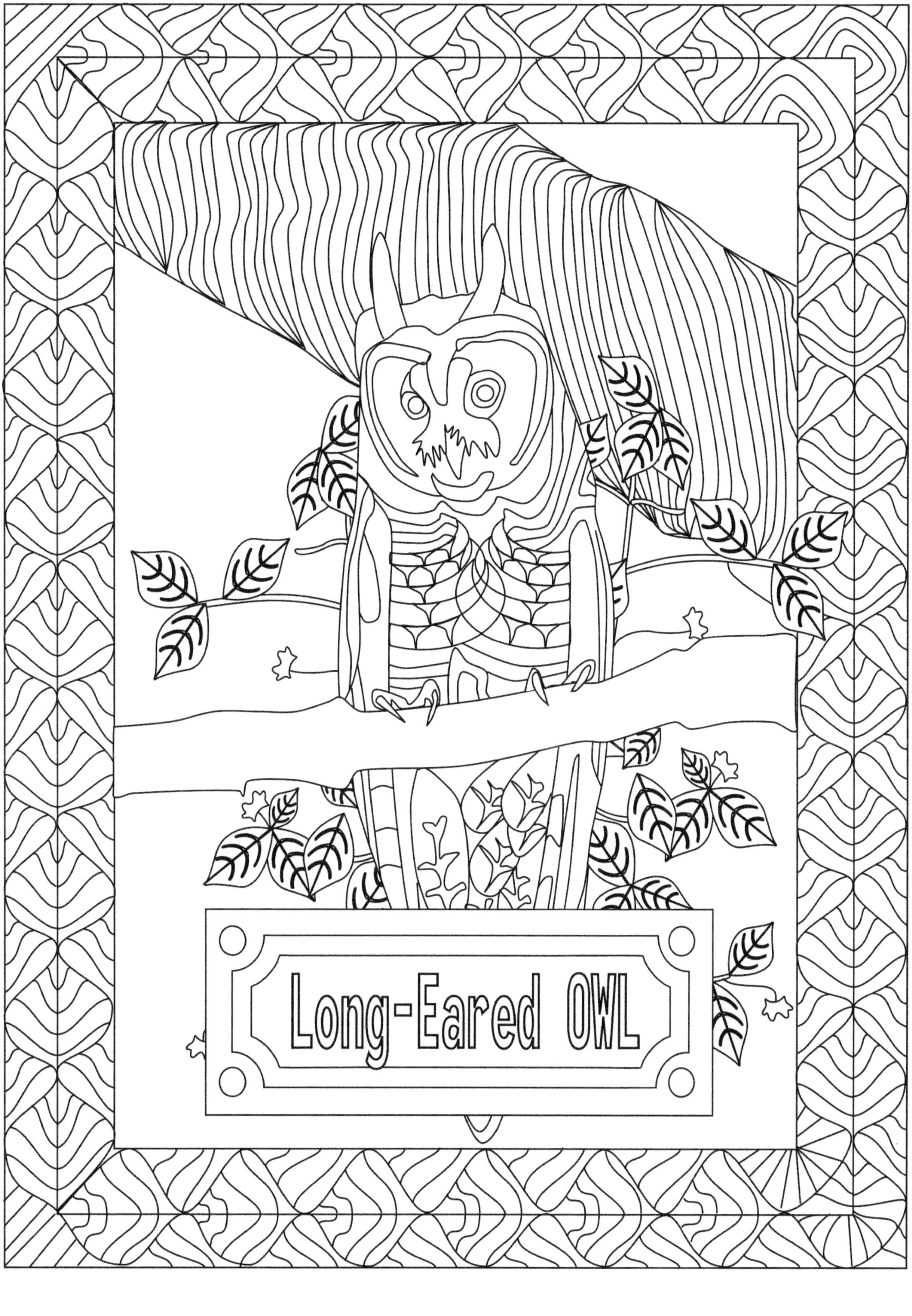
Long-Eared OWL

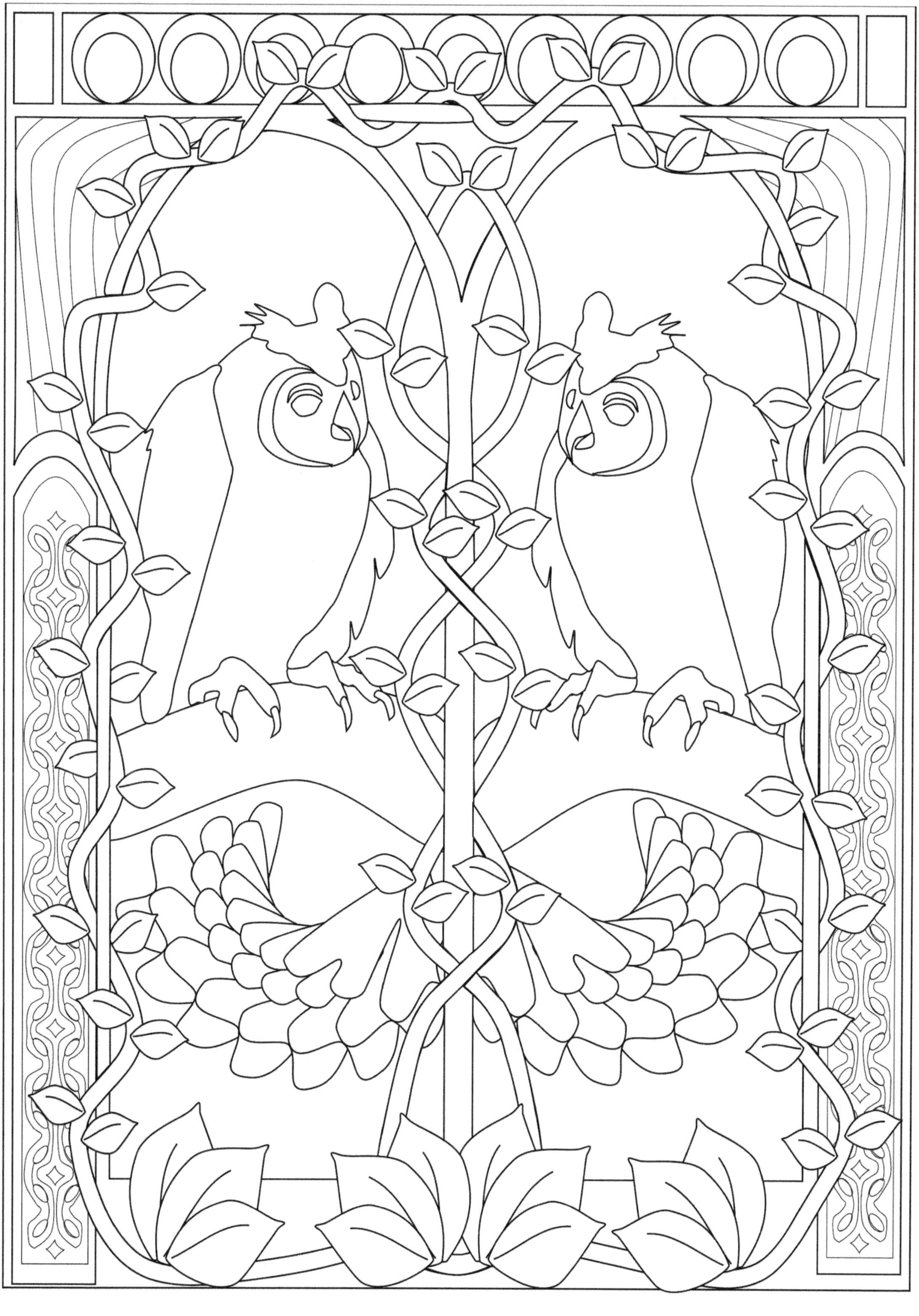

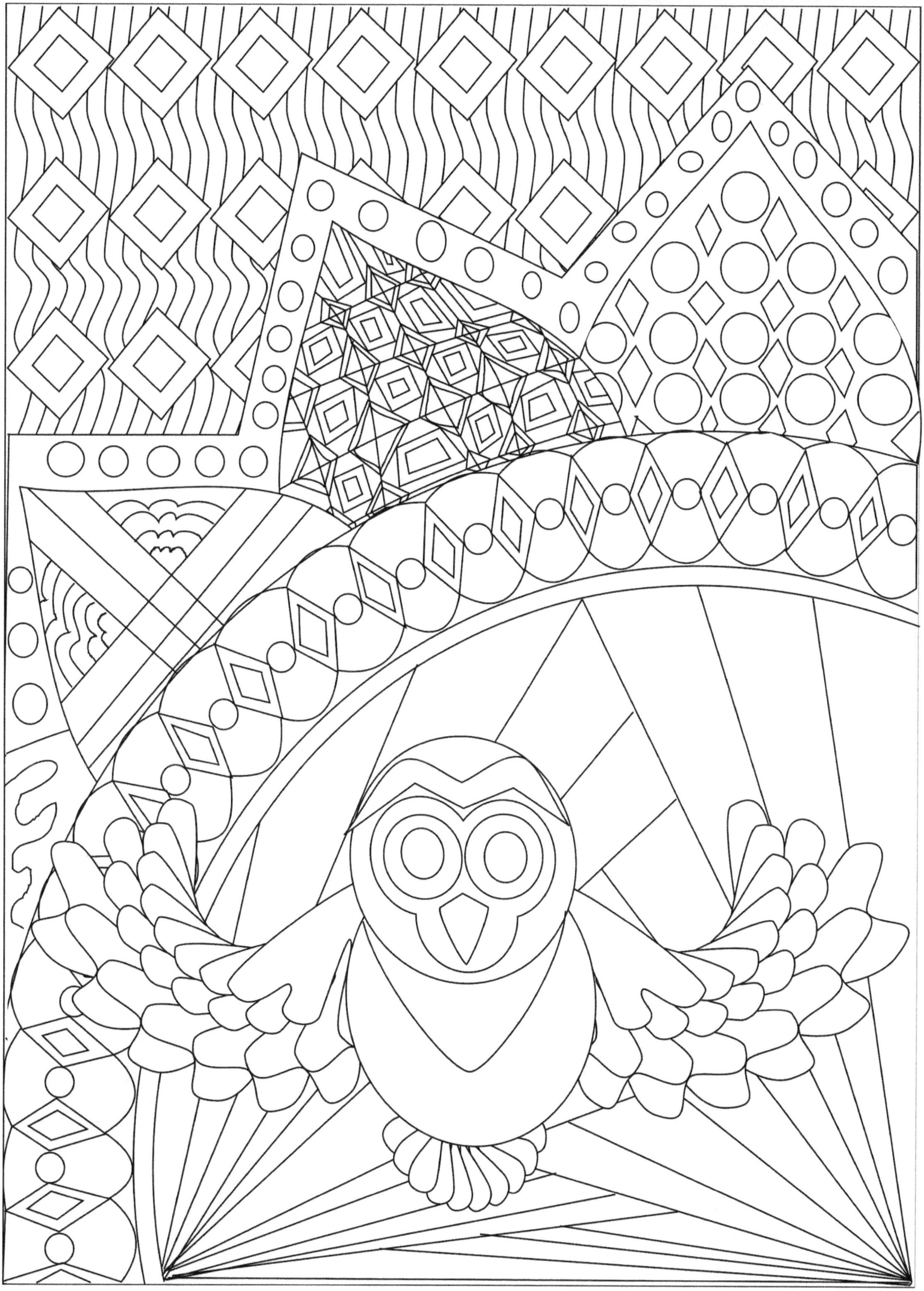

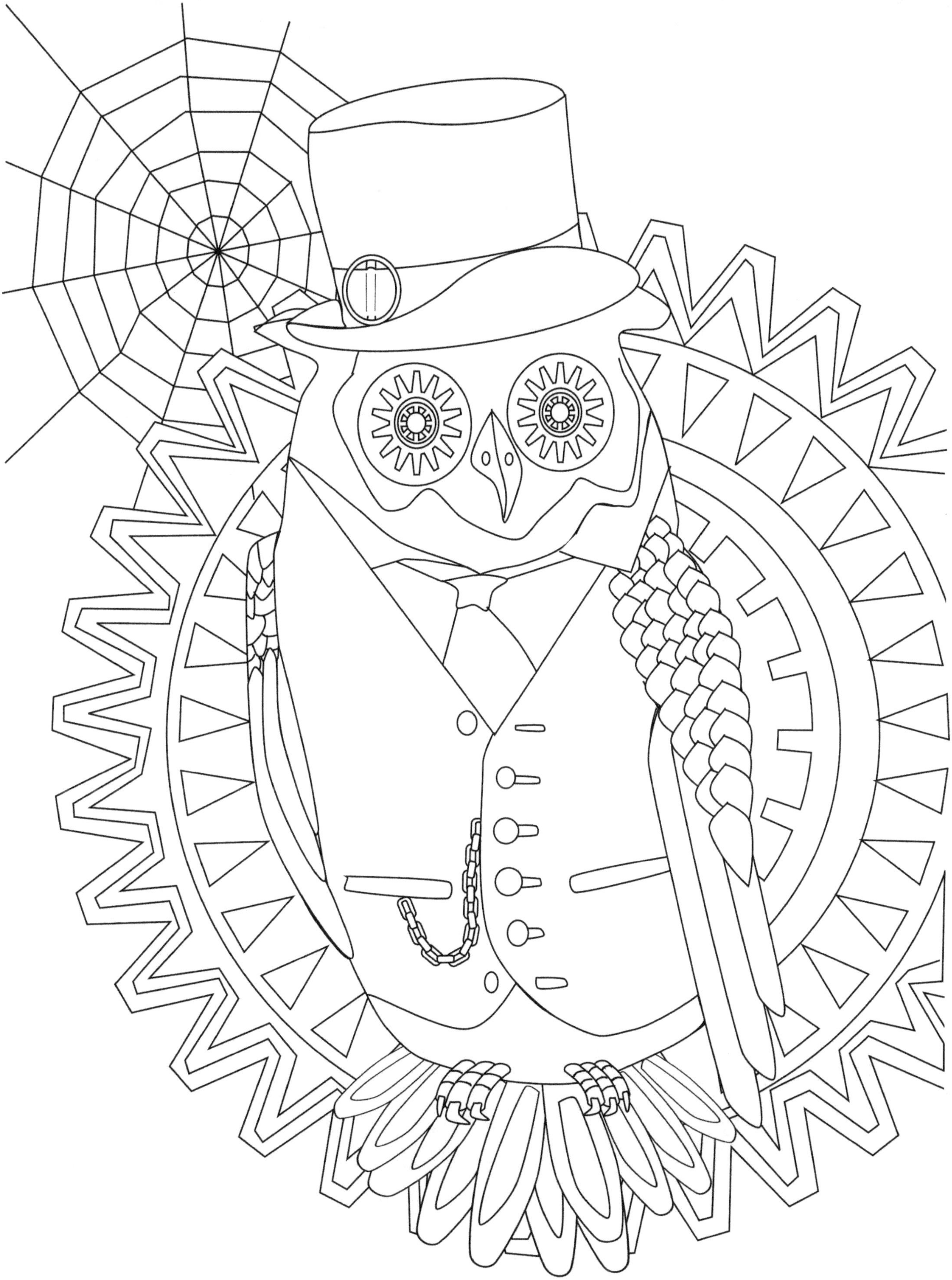

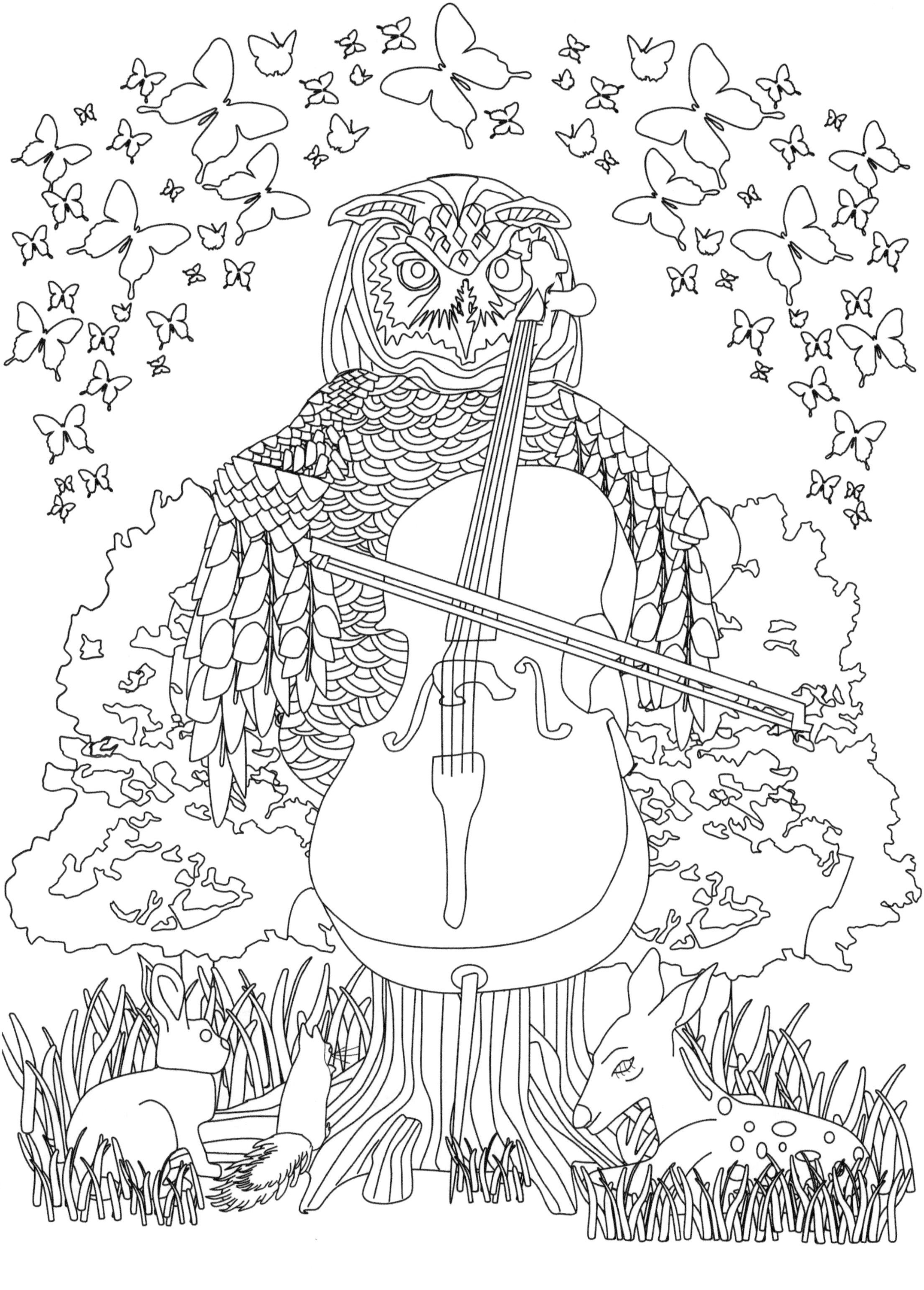

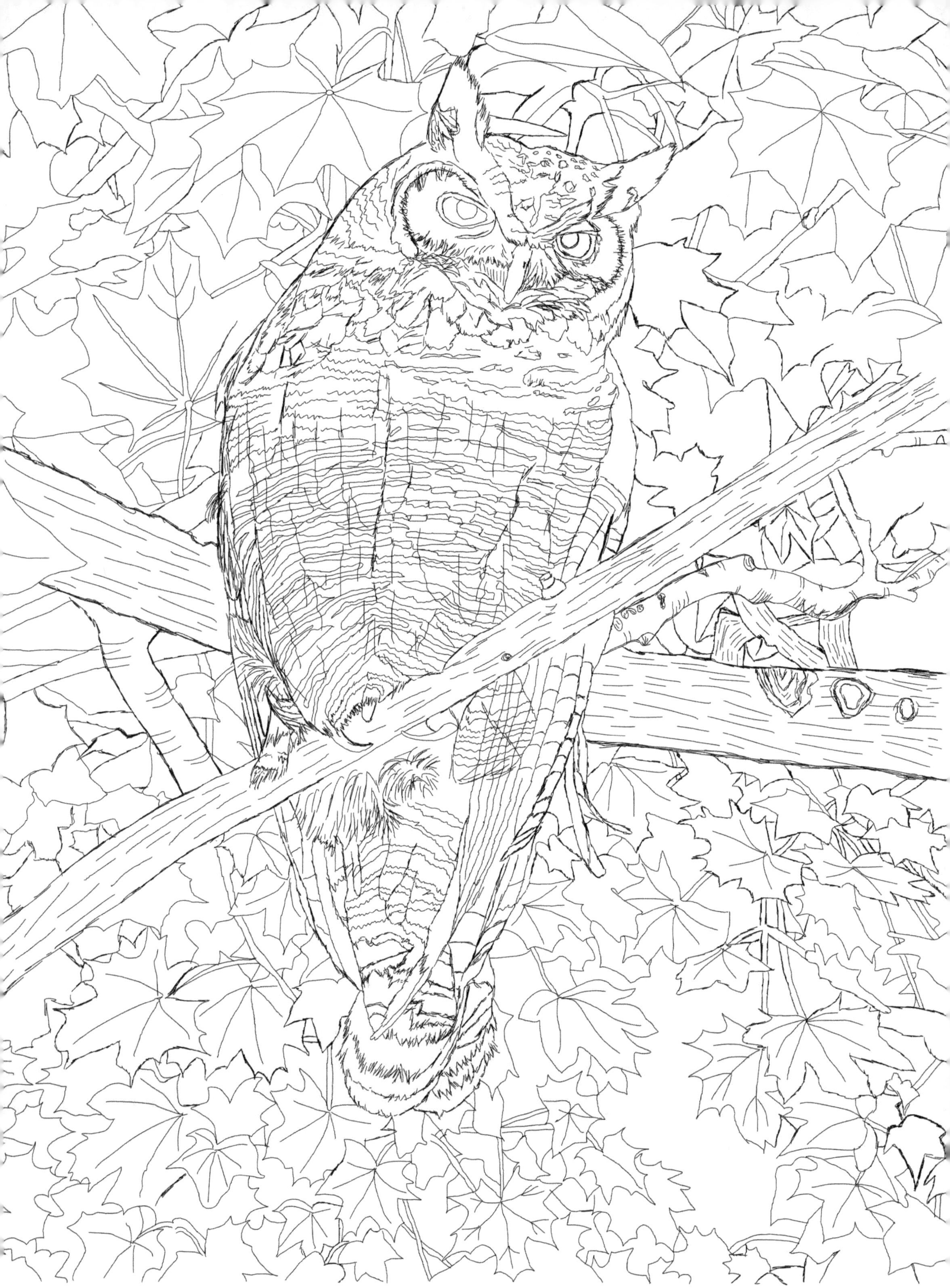

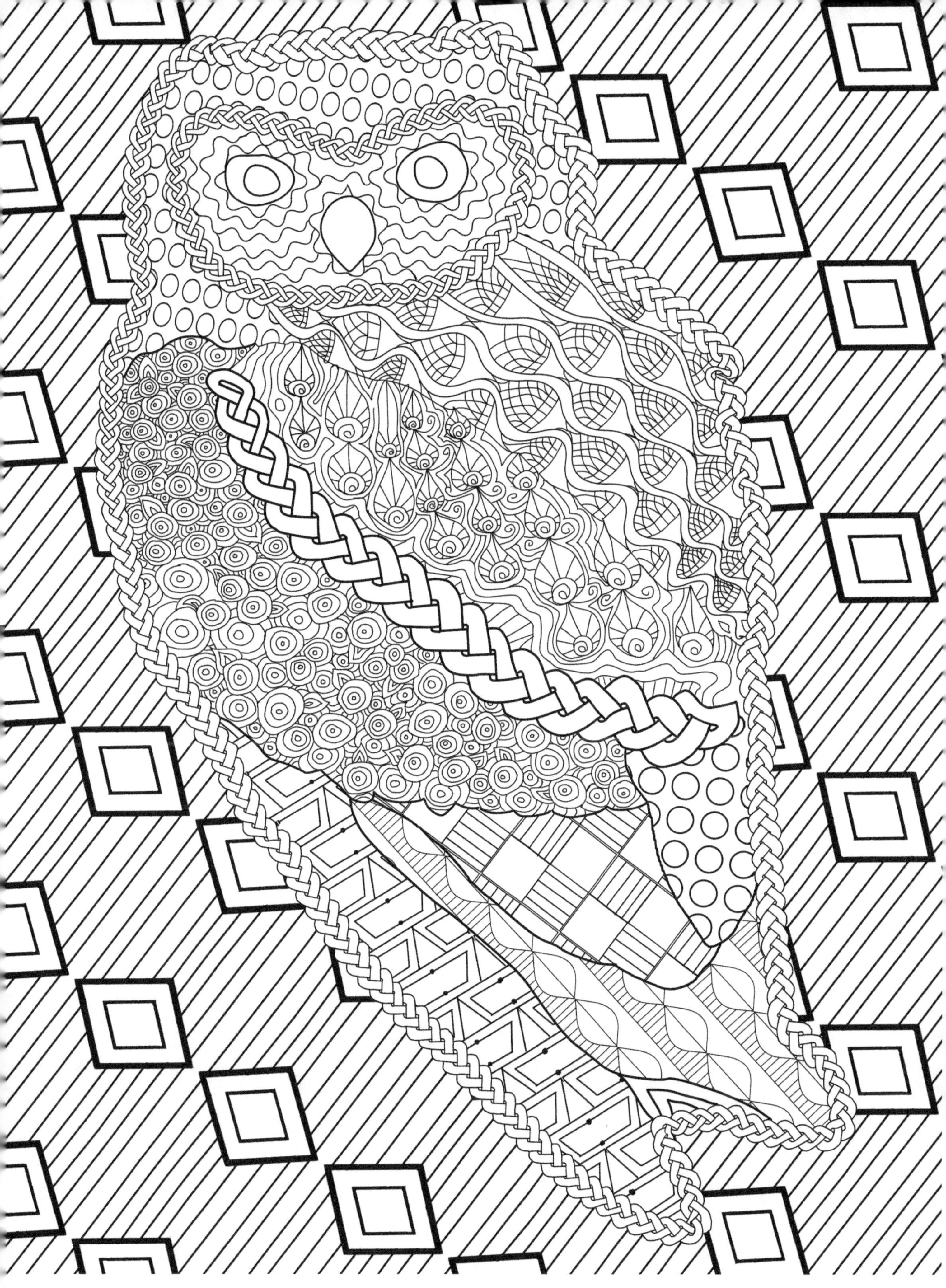

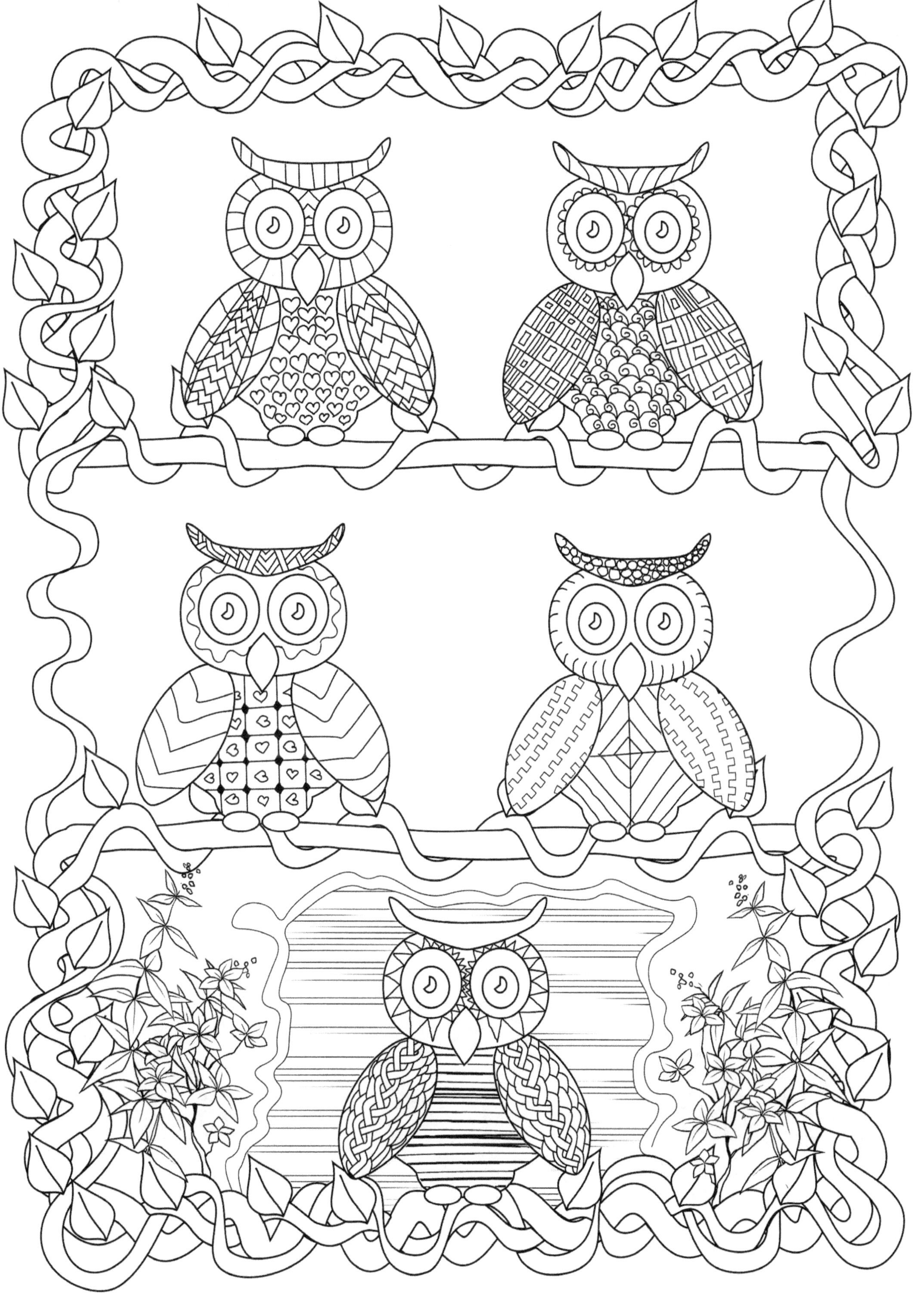

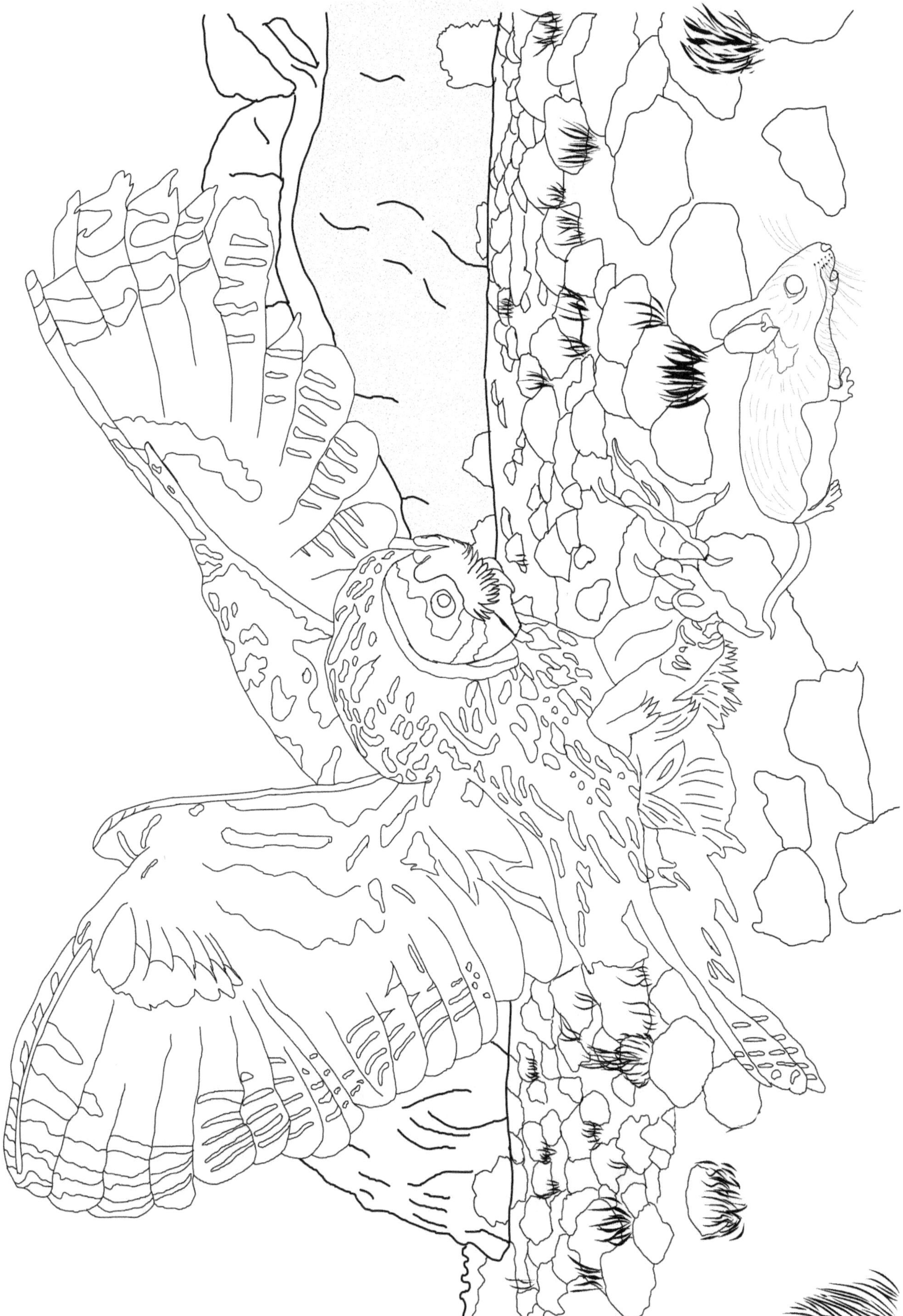

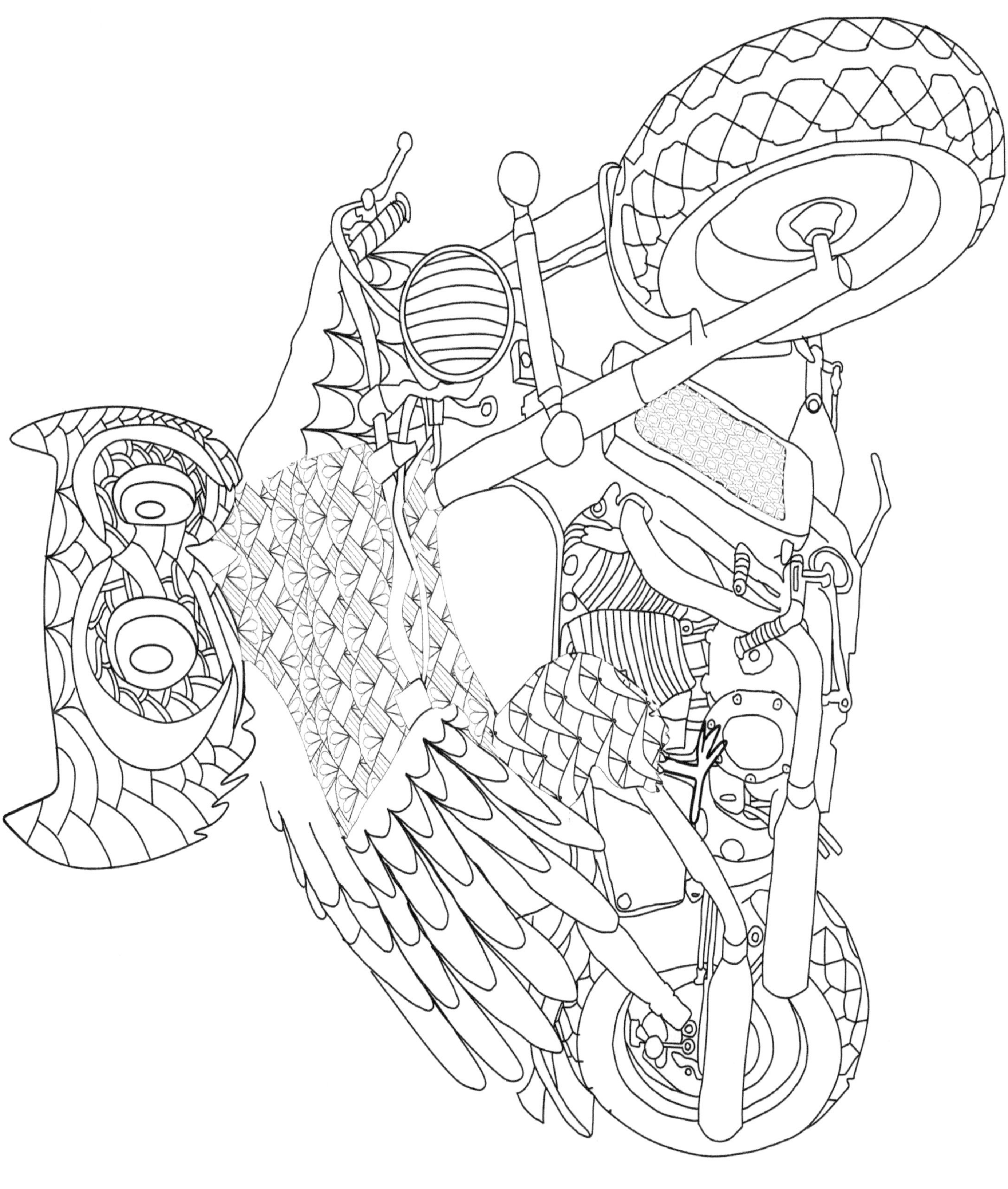

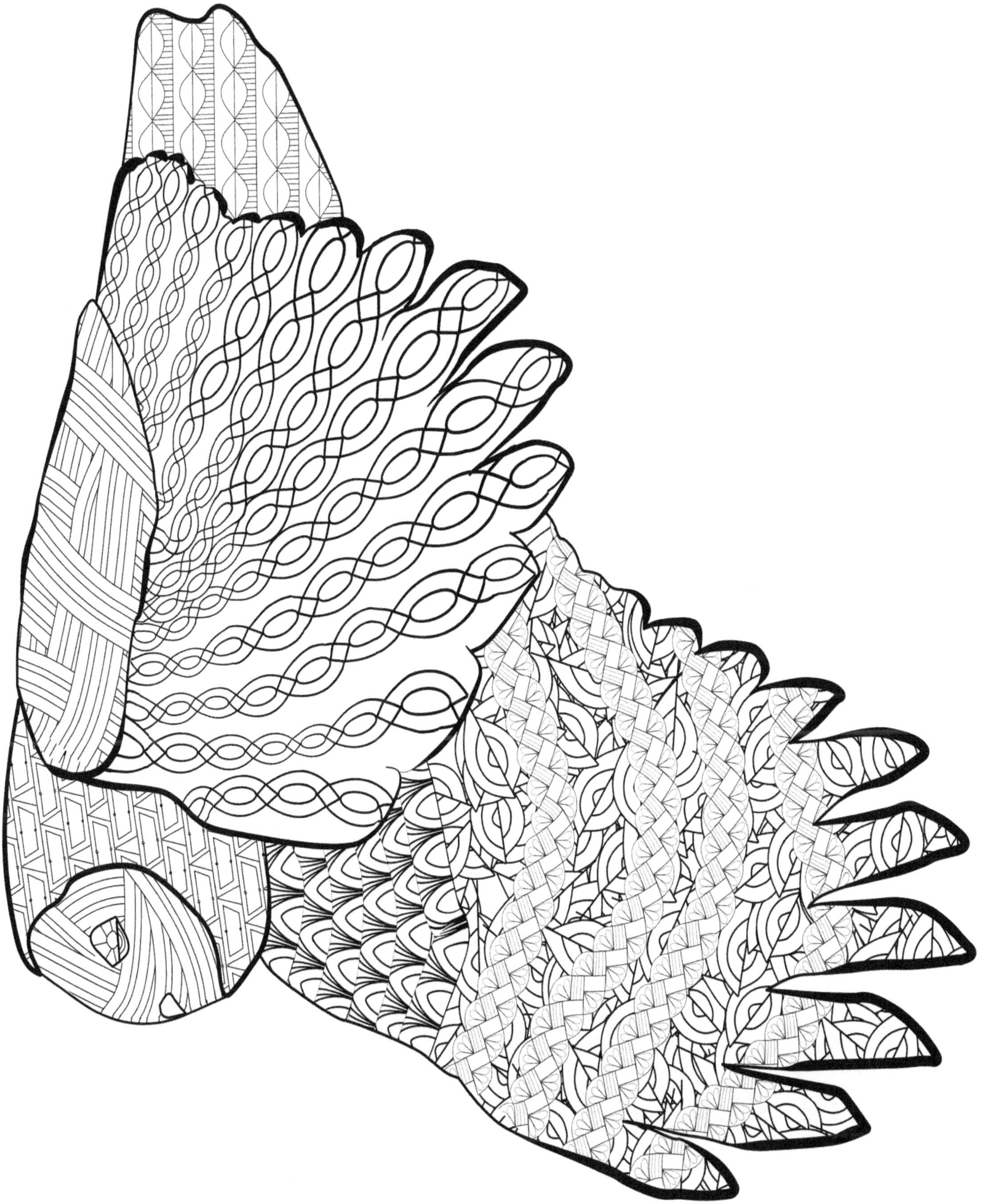

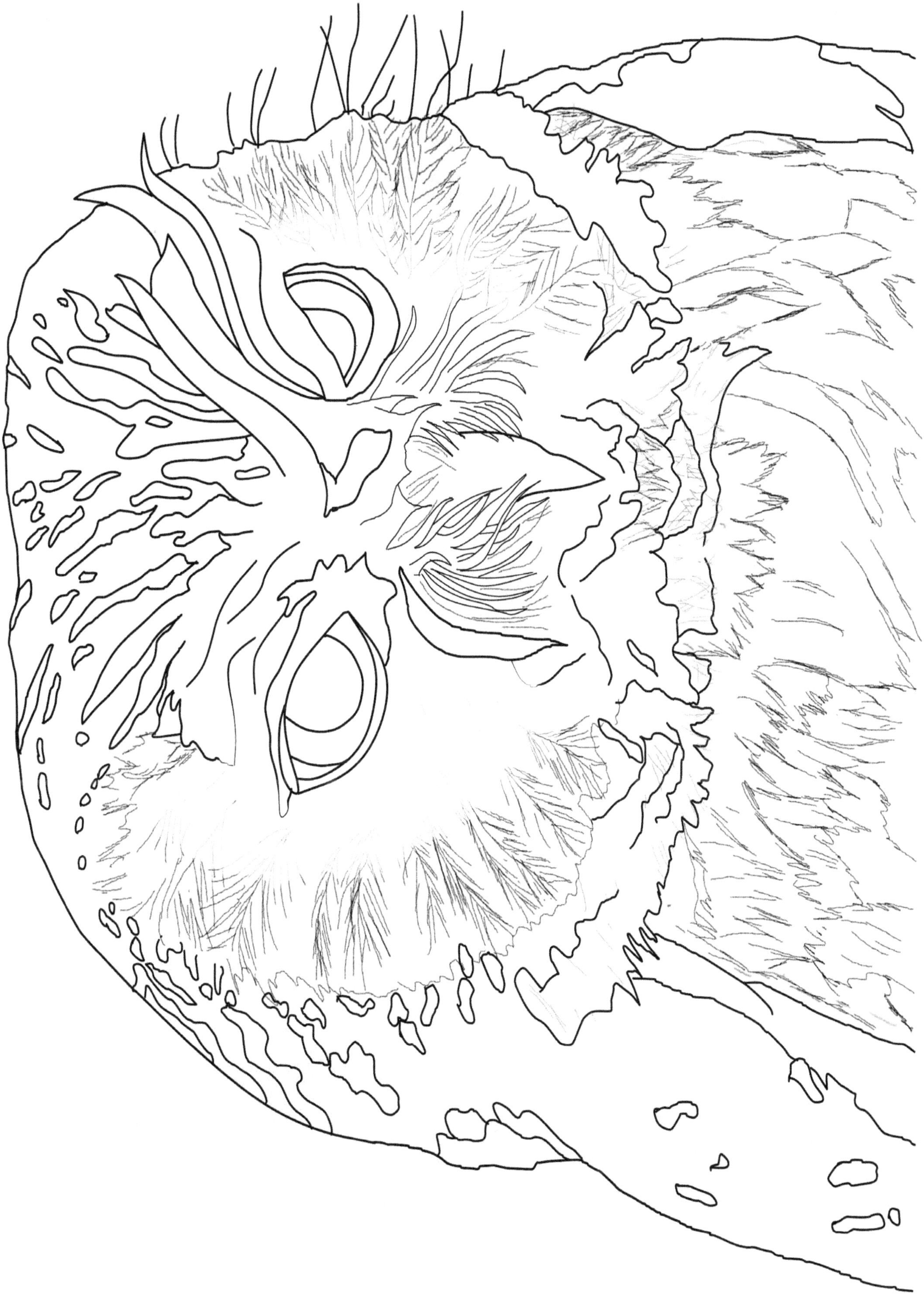

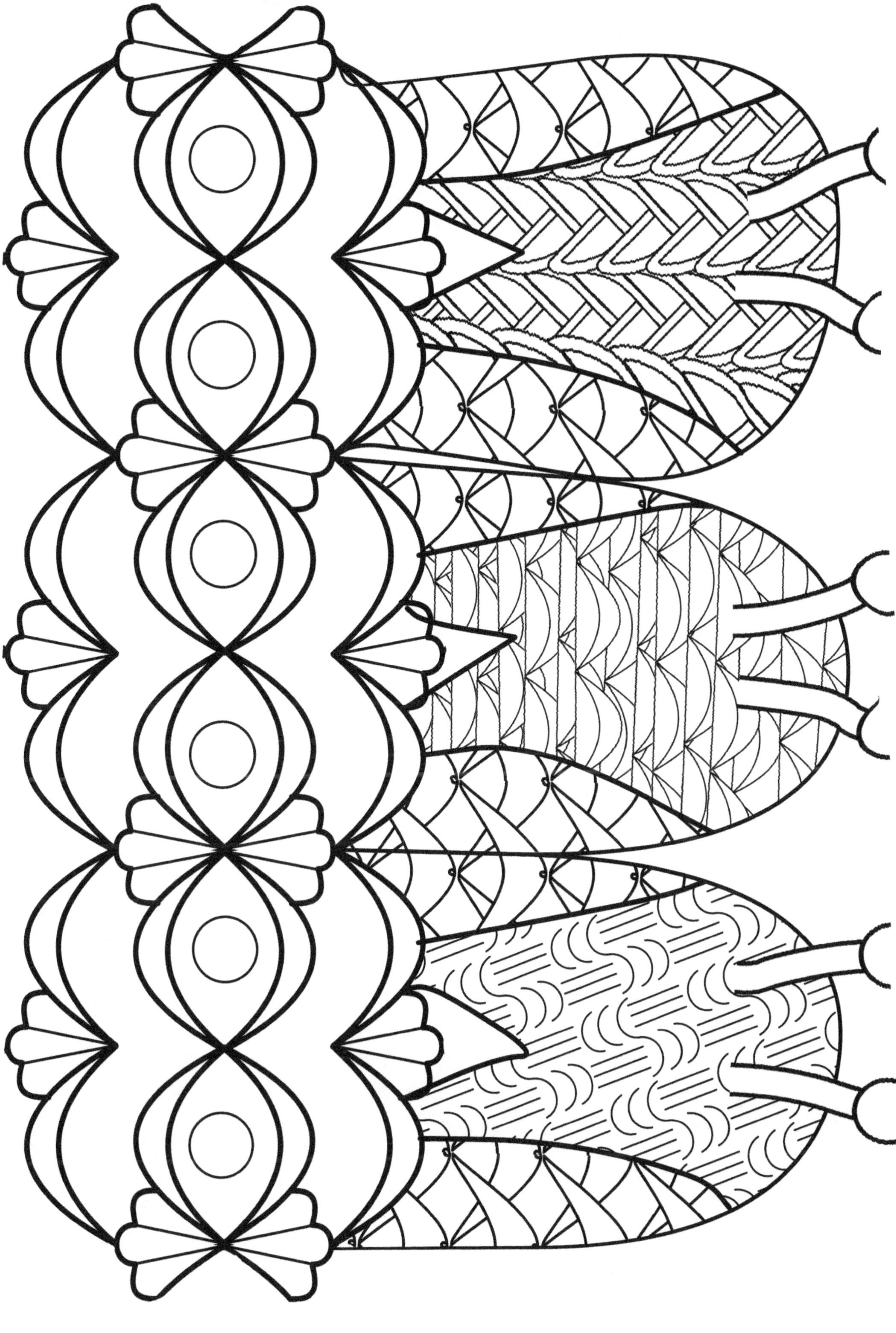

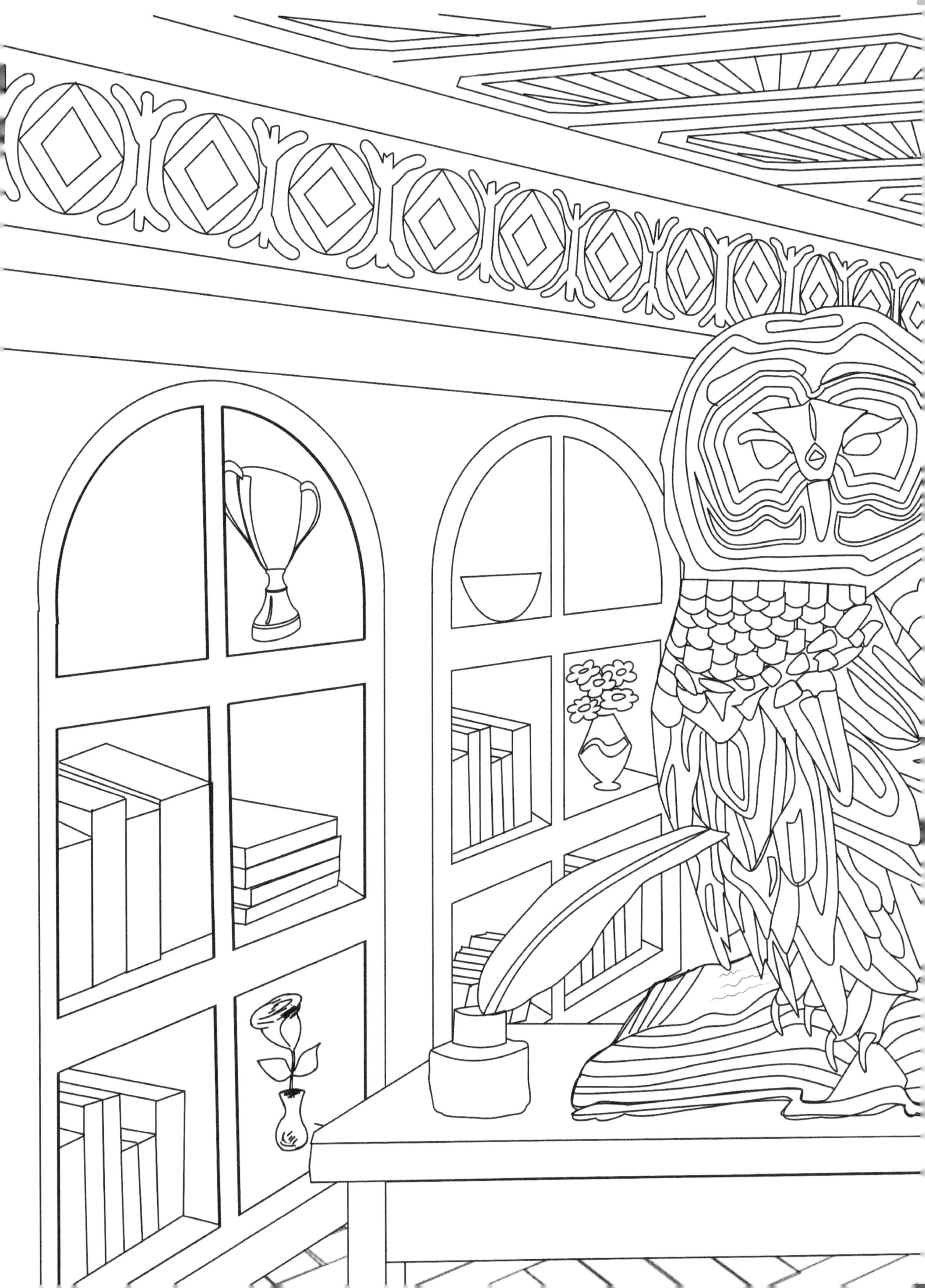

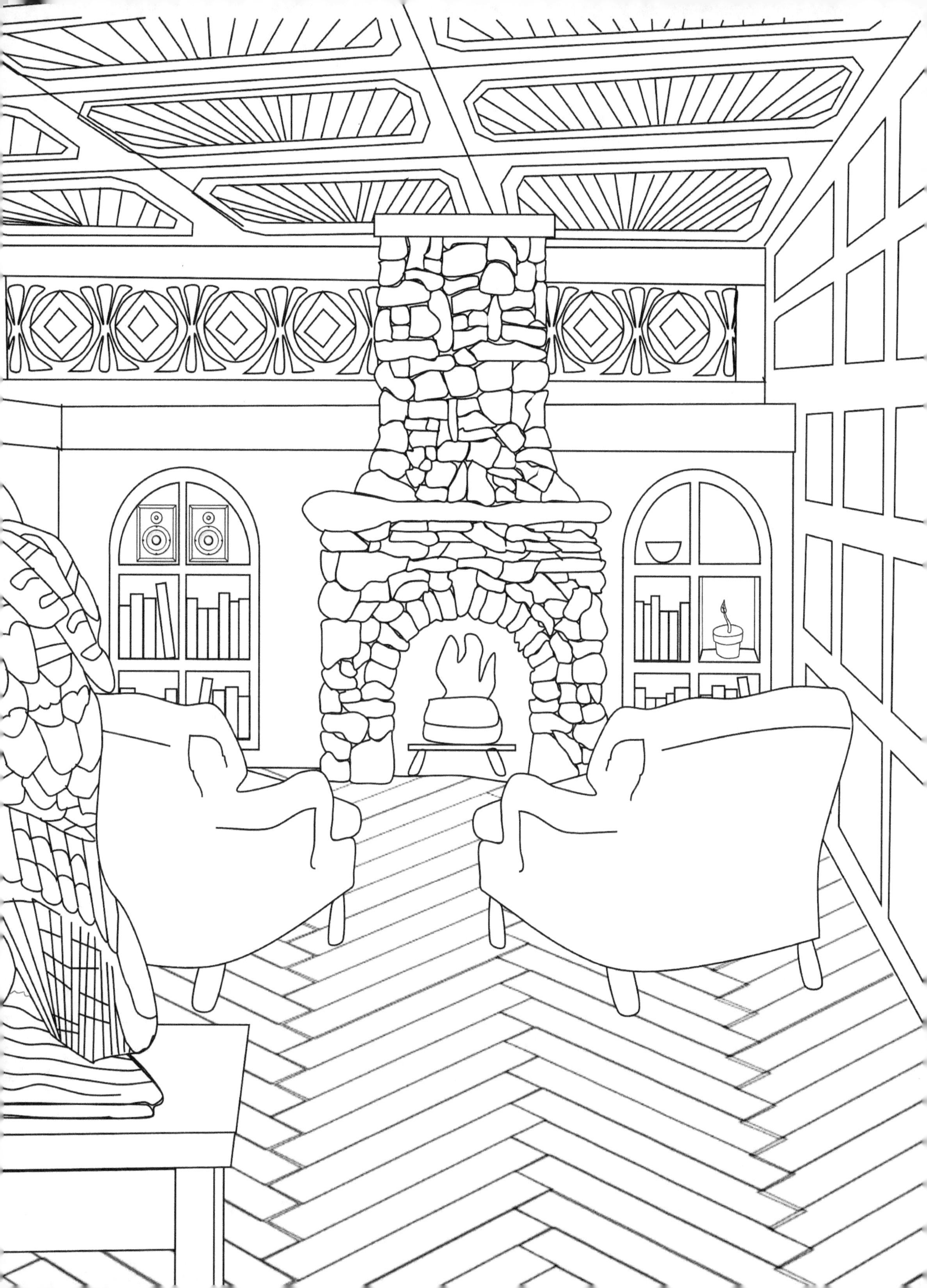

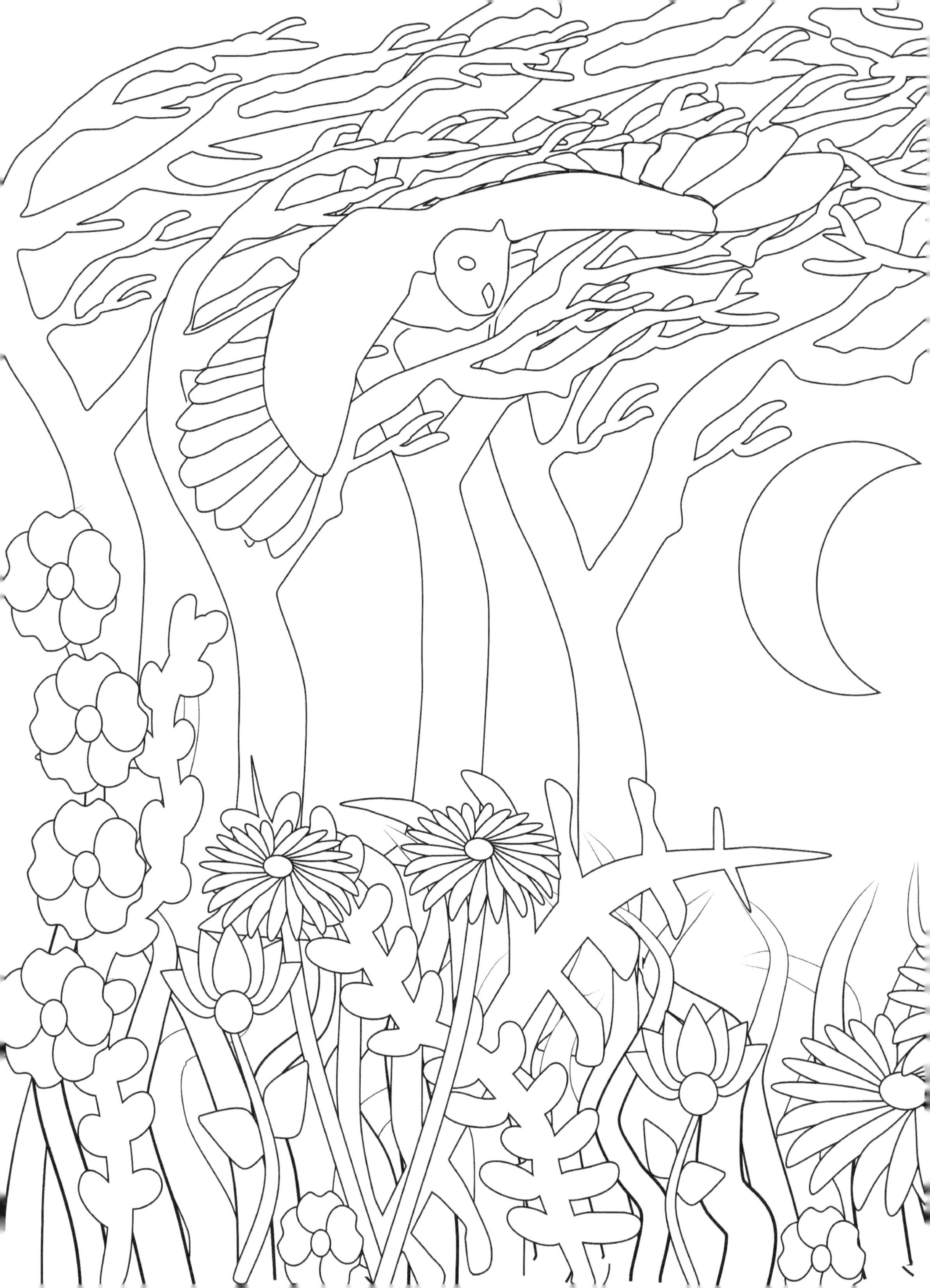

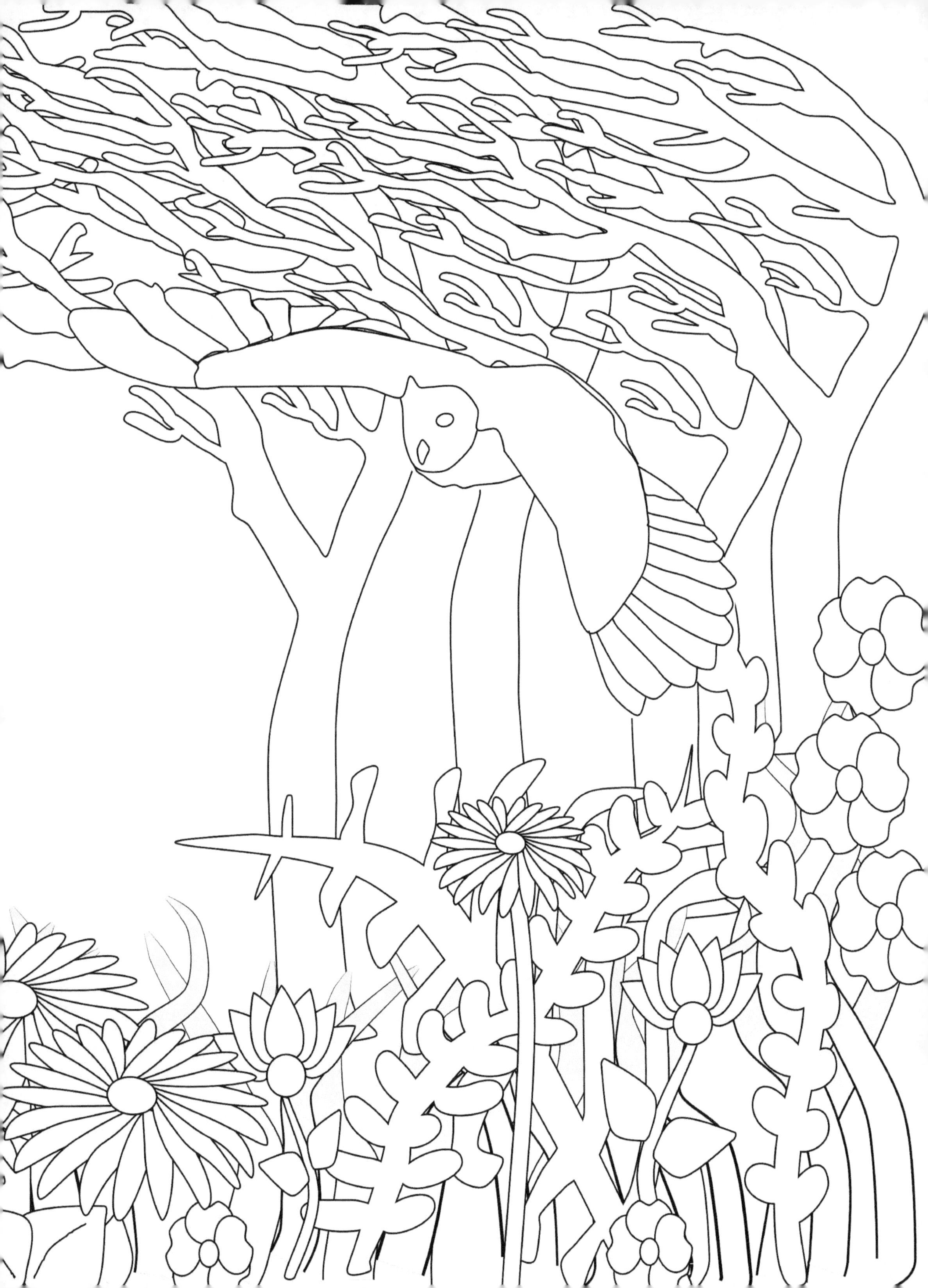

www.ingramcontent.com/pod-product-compliance
Lightning Source LLC
Chambersburg PA
CBHW080547190526
45169CB00007B/2676
9781530462896